Catskill Day Hikes for All Seasons

Catskill Day Hikes
for All Seasons

CAROL AND DAVID WHITE

Adirondack Mountain Club, Inc.
Lake George, New York

Published by the Adirondack Mountain Club, Inc.
814 Goggins Road, Lake George, NY 12845-4117
518-668-4447   www.adk.org

Cover photograph © 2002 by Hardie Truesdale: Looking east from Wittenberg Mountain. Cover design by Ann Hough.
Text design by Christopher Kuntze, adapted by Ann Hough. Text photographs by the authors unless noted otherwise.
Typography by Ann Hough
Maps by The Chazen Companies

Note: Use of the information in this book is at the sole risk of the user.

The Adirondack Mountain Club (ADK) is dedicated to the protection and responsible recreational use of the New York State Forest Preserve, parks, and other wild lands and waters. The Club, founded in 1922, is a member-directed organization committed to public service and stewardship. ADK employs a balanced approach to outdoor recreation, advocacy, environmental education, and natural resource conservation.

Library of Congress Cataloging-in-Publication Data

White, Carol, 1940-
    Catskill day hikes for all seasons / Carol and David White.
        p. cm.
    Includes index.
    ISBN 978-0-935-27254-3 (pbk.)
    1. Hiking—New York (State)—Catskill Mountains—Guidebooks. 2. Trails—New York (State)—Catskill Mountains—Guidebooks. 3. Catskill Mountains (N.Y.)—Guidebooks. I. White, David, 1944- II. Title.

GV199.42.N652 C379 2002
917.47'38044—dc21
                                                                    2002026025

Printed in the United States of America
16 15 14 13   5 6 7 8 9 10

Dedication

This book is dedicated to those far-sighted lovers of nature who created the Catskill and Adirondack "forever wild" Forest Preserve, a magnificent heritage for all the generations to come.

The public lands which constitute the New York State Forest Preserve are unique among all other wild public lands of the United States, in that they enjoy constitutional protection against sale or development. Today, groups such as the Adirondack Mountain Club strive to preserve this precious resource which has provided inspiration for millions of people for over 100 years.

The protection of the Forest Preserve's streams, woodlands, and mountains ultimately rests with you, the individual explorers, who have the responsibility to keep this wondrous resource as pristine as it was when this region's first explorer, Hendrick Hudson, watched the sun fall behind the mountains as he stood aboard the Half Moon *in September 1609.*

We Welcome Your Feedback!

ADK and its authors make every effort to keep our guidebooks up to date; however, trail conditions are always changing. If you note a discrepancy or wish to forward a suggestion, we welcome your comments. Please cite book title, year of your edition and latest printing (see copyright page), trail, page number, and date of your observation. Thanks for your help.

Attention: Publications
Adirondack Mountain Club
814 Goggins Road
Lake George, NY 12845-4117
518-668-4447 ext. 23
pubs@adk.org

Contents

PREFACE   11

USING THIS BOOK   14

BEFORE YOU GO   17

HIKING WITH CHILDREN   23

THE SEASONS   25

THE CATSKILLS   28

Northeast Catskills: North-South Lake and Palenville Area   31
  1. Inspiration Point and Hudson River Valley Lookout   33
  2. Boulder Rock and Split Rock Loop   34
  3. Sunset Rock and Newmans Ledge   36
  4. North Point Loop   38
  5. Sleepy Hollow Trail to Little Pine Orchard Picnic Area   42
  6. Palenville Overlook from Palenville and from South Lake 43
  7. Kaaterskill Falls   46
  8. Catskill Mountain House and Lakeside Loop   47

Northeast Catskills: Blackhead Range
and Northern Escarpment   49
  9. Black Dome Mountain   49
 10. Blackhead Mountain Loop   52
 11. Camels Hump   53
 12. Acra Point and Burnt Knob   55
 13. Windham High Peak   56
 14. Stoppel Point   59
 15. Dutcher Notch from Colgate Lake   61

Northeast Catskills: The Devils Path Peaks   63
 16. West Kill Mountain   64
 17. Hunter Mountain Loops from Spruceton Valley and from Stony Clove 67
 18. Colonels Chair Trail to Hunter Summit   71
 19. Diamond Notch Falls and Diamond Notch   72
 20. Becker Hollow   73
 21. Orchard Point and Dannys Lookout   74
 22. Sugarloaf Mountain Loop   75
 23. Magical Quarry on Sugarloaf   77
 24. Twin Mountain from Pecoy Notch and from Jimmy Dolan Notch   78
 25. Indian Head Mountain Loop   81

East Catskills   85
 26. Kaaterskill High Peak   86
 27. Huckleberry Point   87
 28. Poets Ledge and Wildcat Falls   89

29. Overlook Mountain from Woodstock — 91
30. Echo Lake and Overlook Mountain from Platte Clove — 94
31. Mount Tremper from Willow — 96
32. Onteora Lake — 98
33. Ashokan Reservoir — 101

Central Catskills — 103
34. Belleayre Mountain — 104
35. Cathedral Glen Loop — 106
36. Rochester Hollow — 108
37. Rider Hollow Trail and Balsam Mountain Loop — 109
38. Seager Trail to Waterfalls — 111
39. Lookouts on Dry Brook Ridge — 113
40. Kelly Hollow — 115

South Catskills — 119
41. Slide Mountain Loop via Curtis-Ormsbee Trail — 120
42. Giant Ledge — 122
43. Wittenberg Mountain — 123
44. Wittenberg–Cornell–Slide Loop from Woodland Valley — 125
45. Peekamoose Trail to Overlook Ledge — 126
46. Ashokan High Point — 129
47. Biscuit Brook Bushwhack — 131
48. Red Hill — 133
49. Vernooy Kill Falls — 135

Southwest Catskills — 139
50. Balsam Lake Mountain Loop — 140
51. Alder Lake — 142
52. Little Pond to Touchmenot Mountain View — 143
53. Mongaup Pond and Mountain — 145
54. Frick Pond Loop — 147
55. Covered Bridge Trek to Waterfall — 148
56. Split Rock Lookout — 150
57. Mary Smith Hill — 151
58. Trout Pond and Mud Pond — 154

Northwest Catskills — 157
59. Bearpen Mountain — 158
60. Pratt Rock Park — 160

Appendices
A: Route Difficulty at a Glance — 163
B: Sources and Resources — 164
C: Glossary — 166

About the Authors — 167

Index — 171

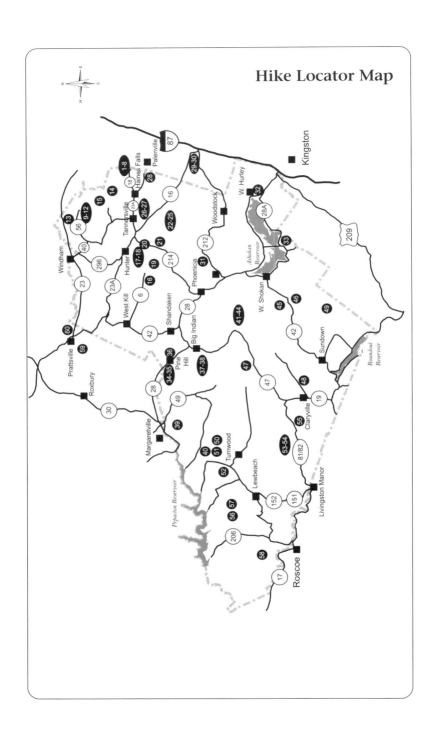

Hike Locator Map

THE CATSKILLS

		PAGE				PAGE
1.	Inspiration Pt.	33		31.	Mount Tremper	96
2.	Boulder Rock, Split Rock	34		32.	Onteora Lake	98
3.	Sunset Rock, Newmans Ledge	36		33.	Ashokan Reservoir	101
4.	North Pt.	38		34.	Belleayre Mt.	104
5.	Little Pine Orchard	42		35.	Cathedral Glen	106
6.	Palenville Overlook	43		36.	Rochester Hollow	108
7.	Kaaterskill Falls	46		37.	Balsam Mt.	109
8.	Catskill Mountain House	47		38.	Seager Trail	111
9.	Black Dome Mt.	49		39.	Dry Brook Ridge	113
10.	Blackhead Mt.	52		40.	Kelly Hollow	115
11.	Camels Hump	53		41.	Slide Mt.	120
12.	Acra Pt., Burnt Knob	55		42.	Giant Ledge	122
13.	Windham High Peak	56		43.	Wittenberg Mt.	123
14.	Stoppel Pt.	59		44.	Wittenberg, Cornell, Slide	125
15.	Dutcher Notch	61		45.	Peekamoose Trail	126
16.	West Kill Mt.	64		46.	Ashokan High Pt.	129
17.	Hunter Mt.	67		47.	Biscuit Brook	131
18.	Colonels Chair Trail	71		48.	Red Hill	133
19.	Diamond Notch Falls	72		49.	Vernooy Kill Falls	135
20.	Becker Hollow	73		50.	Balsam Lake Mt.	140
21.	Orchard Pt.	74		51.	Alder Lake	142
22.	Sugarloaf Mt.	75		52.	Touchmenot Mt.	143
23.	Magical Quarry	77		53.	Mongaup Mt.	145
24.	Twin Mt.	78		54.	Frick Pond	147
25.	Indian Head Mt.	81		55.	Covered Bridge Trek	148
26.	Kaaterskill High Peak	86		56.	Split Rock	150
27.	Huckleberry Pt.	87		57.	Mary Smith Hill	151
28.	Poets Ledge	89		58.	Trout Pond, Mud Pond	154
29.	Overlook Mt.	91		59.	Bearpen Mt.	158
30.	Echo Lake	94		60.	Pratt Rock Park	160

Top of Diamond Notch Falls

Preface

Recently we met three hikers on Orchard Point atop Plateau Mountain, one getting in shape for climbing in Switzerland by hiking twelve miles of the Devil's Path, which includes 4,275 feet of elevation gain over four mountains.

"The Catskills are tremendously underrated as challenging mountains," one was saying.

"These mountains are at least as good as others in the Northeast!" another agreed.

It reminded us of "The Catskills: A New Englander's Perspective" by Bob Parlee, written for the Catskill 3500 Club's *Catskill Canister*. "I'm truly shocked that more New Englanders haven't discovered these fine mountains," he writes.

Parlee has hiked for over 20 years throughout New England and New York, and when he mentions the Catskills the typical response is, "Isn't that a hilly place with a lot of big hotels?"

He describes the Catskills' summit vistas, the cliffside views from the escarpment, the diversity of forest and wildlife. "I feel lucky and privileged to be a New Englander who loves the Catskills. To me, the Catskills truly represent our eastern mountains," he concludes.

As central New Yorkers, we plead guilty to the same initial oversight. We used to think *Adirondacks* when we planned to hike. One day on Pitchoff Mountain in the Adirondack High Peaks, we met a couple from New Jersey who told us about some of the best trails in the Catskills.

We headed south and were soon hooked by the many challenging ascents in the Catskills. We climbed 35 mountains over 3500 feet, a requirement of the Catskill 3500 Club. Membership also requires climbing four of those peaks in *winter*! Wasn't this pursuit only for "extreme" hikers? We thought that investing in snowshoes wasn't a bad idea anyway; with trepidation, we also bought crampons.

We climbed Slide, Panther, Balsam, and Blackhead Mountains between December and March, and became more and more awestruck. Little on earth compares to the beauty and invigoration of a trek up a snow-blanketed mountainside, sunlight transforming fresh powder into sparkling jewels and lighting up ice-covered branches that clink together in the breeze. We are grateful for that winter requirement, for it introduced us to our favorite season to hike the mountains.

We began discovering other wonders in the Catskill Forest Preserve. The 23-mile Escarpment Trail is fascinating, entailing hiking along the Great Wall of Manitou, a formidable 1600-foot cliff rising out of the Hudson River Valley. This rugged trail is the site of an annual marathon that starts near Windham and continues all the way to North-South Lake!

We discovered the Long Path, which winds through the Catskills for 95 miles, over peaks and along ridges, by waterfalls and lookout ledges. A new trail has been cut from the Long Path to Poet's Ledge, which overhangs Kaaterskill Clove, "the land of falling waters."

We explored informal trails such as the path up to the Burroughs Range by the Neversink River, and the south approach to Kaaterskill High Peak's lookout ledge, where one can see a wrecked airplane on the snowmobile trail. We traversed wooded ridges when leaves were off the trees, allowing splendid views. We wrote stories about ten of our winter climbs and, somewhere along the way, we proposed a book of hikes.

* * *

Catskill Day Hikes is intended to introduce you to the incomparable region of rugged natural beauty known as the Catskill Park, still wild and pristine after 400 years of American development. Our descriptions comprise a selection of waterfalls, mountain summits, wilderness lakes, escarpment cliffs, cascading streams, and beautiful lookouts.

This book was written to serve a wide range of users. Thus we prepared material for those new to hiking or to the Catskills, while also including hikes for those whose outdoor experience is considerable. We include a mix of easy, moderate, and strenuous hikes, often describing further options.

Catskill Day Hikes features destinations within reach by foot in a day trip or an hour, with commentary on seasonal aspects of the trails. Most treks are on established trails, often combining parts of several trails to make an interesting loop. In contrast, the Adirondack Mountain Club (ADK) *Guide to Catskill Trails* gives a comprehensive, end-to-end description for every trail in the Catskills, allowing the hiker to choose his or her own experience. It includes backpacking and off-trail (bushwhacking) suggestions.

Thanks to work on this book, we are still discovering trails, lakes, summits, rushing brooks, overlook ledges, and beautiful forests throughout the Catskill Park.

* * *

We wish to thank the following people:

Bill and Patti Rudge, for their ready assistance and advice.

Bruce C. Wadsworth and the Schenectady Chapter of the Adirondack Mountain Club, for undertaking the immense task of planning and writing the first edition of the comprehensive *Guide to Catskill Trails*, published by the Adirondack Mountain Club.

Anthony Amaral Jr., John P. (Jack) Freeman, Darielle Graham, and Claudia Swain for reviewing this manuscript and making many helpful comments and suggestions.

Timothy Hack and Meghan Hayes, for photographing the Devil's Path west of Sugarloaf, perhaps the most interesting and rugged trail in the Catskills, after we ran out of film.

Gene Ligotti, whose series on the Catskills in the *Catskill Mountain Region Guide* offers interesting insights and facts into the history and geography of the region.

Brian Sullivan, for much helpful correspondence with ADK about conditions and changes in the Catskill Forest Preserve.

Using This Book

The trails described in this book are nearly all within the Catskill Forest Preserve, the state land within the Catskill Park (see Blue Line Matters box).

Time and distance. Because of individual differences and preferences in hiking styles, we do not give an estimated travel time for each hike. Instead, distance and elevation-change data are provided at the beginning of each hike description. We suggest you take a conservative approach by allowing one hour for every 1.5 miles plus 30 minutes for each 1000 feet of ascent.

Your experience will indicate how close you are to this standard. Don't expect descents, especially on steep trails, to be quicker than ascents. Accidents happen when people hurry on the way out.

Difficulty. This rating, too, is found in the information provided at the start of each description and should be noted and compared with your own experience. "Moderate" for a young or physically fit person may be "strenuous" for a novice or an unconditioned person. Trip ratings are for level of effort to be expended. Difficult trail conditions are noted also.

Blue Line Matters

The "blue line" that defines the Adirondack and Catskill Parks is said to have originated in 1891 when politicians and others proposing the creation of the Adirondack Park outlined its boundaries in blue ink on a New York State map. The term was later extended to the Catskill Park. Today these parks are a patchwork of public and private lands that brings at least as much confusion as joy to residents and visitors alike.

The Forest Preserve comprises the public or state-owned lands, a little less than half the total land area of these parks. This distinction matters to the average hiker because the extensive trails in both parks rely on a combination of public lands and rights-of-way granted by private landowners. In addition, the official designations—Wilderness, Wild Forest, Primitive Area, etc.—have their own attendant regulations.

With few exceptions, the trails described in this book are located on public lands. Where parts of the trails or the trailhead itself is on private land, the owners have given permission for traverse by the hiking public. On these trails and elsewhere in these unique parks, hikers must respect private landowners' rights and abide by the conditions of use in order to retain the privilege of access.

These ratings are necessarily subjective, although we have attempted to standardize the use of terms relating to steepness and overall difficulty. Appendix A, Route Difficulty at a Glance, lists all of the hikes in this book in alphabetical order according to the difficulty rating for each. Because some hike descriptions include an option—an extended loop, for example—the main hike described may appear in one difficulty category while a longer, more strenuous loop option would be listed elsewhere. We suggest you use Appendix A to assist you in choosing hikes and in evaluating your experience of a particular trail relative to the book's trail ratings overall.

Trails in the Catskills tend to start climbing almost immediately and then level off on ridge tops, where they become long enjoyable rambles. Take your time in the early stages of a hike until the terrain levels. The lengthy switchbacks common in the western United States, which make a stubborn grade into a pleasant stroll, are quite rare in New York State.

Maps. Every trail description in this book has a corresponding map referenced by page number in the summary information. Public-private land boundaries are shown only where they are specifically mentioned in the text as features to be attentive to, usually by way of avoiding trespass. The legend for these page maps follows:

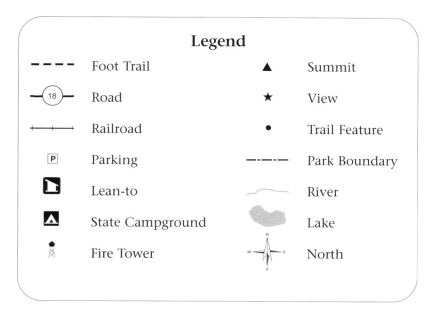

Legend

┈┈┈	Foot Trail	▲	Summit
—(18)—	Road	★	View
┼——┼	Railroad	●	Trail Feature
P	Parking	┈·┈·	Park Boundary
◧	Lean-to	⌒	River
◭	State Campground	⬭	Lake
🗼	Fire Tower	✳	North

Also referenced are the five Catskill Forest Preserve trail maps, titled *Catskill Trails*, published by the New York-New Jersey Trail Conference. The set includes:

North Lake Area Catskill Trails, Map 40

Northeastern Catskill Trails, Map 41

Central Catskill Trails, Map 42

Southern Catskill Trails, Map 43

Western Catskill Trails, Map 44

They can be purchased from ADK by calling 800-395-8080 (8:30 A.M.–5:00 P.M., Monday–Saturday) or from the New York–New Jersey Trail Conference, 156 Ramapo Valley Road, Mahwah, NJ 07430.

Because many Catskill trailheads are off the beaten track, we recommend acquiring the *New York State Atlas and Gazetteer*, by the DeLorme Mapping Company, although it does have some errors.

Each hike summary also lists the United States Geological Survey (USGS) 7.5-minute series topographic maps. Their larger scale is useful to hikers who wish to explore off-trail. These maps are available in English and metric measurements from bookstores, outdoor retailers, and the USGS (for more info about USGS products: www.usgs.gov or 800-USA-MAPS).

We have hiked most of these trails many times, and hiked all of them again prior to publication of this book, in order to describe each in detail. With alertness to one's surroundings, trails in the Catskills are easy to follow. However, we have noted conditions that can be disorienting, such as recent blowdown from storms, markers chewed by porcupines or obscured by growing tree-bark, areas with sparse trail markers, beaver flooding, leafy or snow-covered trails, rocky sections, and areas in evergreen forests where the trail is vague. Hikers should stay alert for changes of direction, usually signaled by double trail markers, with the top one indicating the direction

"Batteries Not Included"

Global Positioning System (GPS) receivers and (more often) cell phones are gaining ever-larger followings, and their popularity has met with both glee and deep chagrin. Philosophical matters aside, hikers carrying these should ask themselves if they are prepared to be without them.

Reliance on devices that require batteries poses a danger in the wilderness, where there isn't a "corner store." Reception is strongly influenced by the very features we go to the mountains to enjoy: remoteness and dramatic topography. Finally, these devices often impart a false sense of security that can lead hikers to go beyond their abilities and assume they can rely on securing assistance if they get into trouble.

change. Before proceeding too far without trail markers, return to the last place you saw one.

Mileage is generally accurate to within one-tenth of a mile. Sometimes a Department of Environmental Conservation (DEC) trail sign shows a mileage different from one found here. Because ADK guides are revised more often than DEC signs, we suggest you rely on this guide. Short distances are expressed in yards.

The Catskills' five remaining fire towers are now completely renovated. The Adirondack Mountain Club Information Center at Lake George is a good source for updates, as is the Club's *Views from on High: Fire Tower Trails in the Adirondacks and Catskills*, by John P. Freeman. Information Center staff and the ADK Web site (www.adk.org) are good sources also for learning about ADK's Fire Tower Challenge.

Before You Go

The following section offers some time-tested advice.

Tell someone your plans, including your destination and approximate time of return. Sign in at the trailhead register, and sign out upon your return. DEC forest rangers consult this information to monitor overall trail use and search for overdue hikers.

Bring a topographical map and a compass. (For more about maps, see Using This Book.) Plan to leave as much time for walking out as for going in; injuries are likely to occur when rushing at dusk, especially when going downhill. The sedimentary rock of the Catskills is more slippery than rock elsewhere.

Watch the weather and wear or take appropriate clothing. Check the local weather report, but remember that mountain weather can quickly change for the worse (or the better). Every hiker should be familiar with the warning signs of hypothermia and heat exhaustion.

Hypothermia is a lowered body core temperature that occurs most often when the air temperature is between thirty and fifty degrees. The first signs are involuntary shivering, slowing of pace, and loss of coordination such as stumbling, slurred speech, and disorientation. Get high-energy, quickly-digested food and hot drink into the person. Warm the person in any way possible; if untreated, hypothermia can be fatal.

Normally, the body's own thermostat keeps you comfortable and regulates body temperature. On hot, humid days with little breeze, the body works hard to maintain that internal temperature. Be aware of the symptoms of heat exhaustion: heavy sweating, weakness, cold, pale, and clammy skin, weak pulse, fainting, and vomiting. Lie down in a cool, shaded place and loosen clothing. Apply wet cloths to the skin and have moderate drinks of water. Heat stroke is more serious and requires medical attention. It is characterized by mental confusion, chills, dizziness, and loss of consciousness. Body temperature often reaches 105 degrees, the skin is hot and dry, and the pulse is fast and strong.

Prevention is the wisest strategy. Decrease the intensity of exercise on hot, humid days, and drink plenty of water before, during, and after your hike. Wear lightweight, loose, breathable clothing. A wet bandanna can help keep you cool.

Good physical conditioning is essential in order to enjoy hiking, and is the best way to prevent accidents and aches. Aerobic workouts such as jogging, brisk walking, biking, or swimming four days a week increase the heart's efficiency. Capillaries that carry oxygen and nutrients from the blood to muscle cells increase in number with regular exercise. Muscle cells improve at using this "fuel." Beneficial changes start immediately. Get a book on aerobic exercise, weight training, and yoga for top fitness.

Who're Ya Gonna Call?

Emergency calls should be directed to 911, according to the New York State Department of Environmental Conservation (DEC). The 911 dispatchers can contact the appropriate DEC forest ranger or other emergency personnel.

Alternatively, emergency calls can be directed as follows:
• DEC Region 3 (Ulster and Sullivan Counties): 845-256-3000 during normal business hours; at other times call New Paltz Police Dispatch 845-255-1323.
• DEC Region 4 (Delaware and Greene Counties): 607-652-5076/5063 and 518-357-2161, respectively. On weekends and after hours, call the New York State Police in Ulster County (Kingston, 845-338-1702), Sullivan County (Liberty, 845-292-6600), Greene County (Catskill-Cairo, 518-622-8600), or Delaware County (Margaretville, 845-586-2681). Or call the Sheriff's Department in Delhi at 607-746-2336.

Note: Queries, information, and concerns also can be directed to the pertinent DEC numbers cited above.

Clothing. Cotton clothing should be avoided on the trail, because it absorbs moisture, does not dry, and clings to the body. In windy weather with dropping temperature, it can be uncomfortable and dangerous. The key to control of heat and cold is layering of clothes. Many new hikers tend to overdress, leading to excess perspiration. The shirt closest to the body should be breathable and quick-drying, such as polypropylene or a cotton/polypropylene mix. Consider vests as a light next layer, plus wool or fleece shirts, sweaters, or jackets for further warmth. Even on a sunny day, carry a breathable Gore-Tex shell or nonplastic rain gear.

Take off layers as the body heats up, and add them when necessary. Having those extra layers can be important, too, in case of emergency and enforced hours of inactivity. At least forty percent of body heat is lost through the head. Getting hot while climbing? Take your hat off. Feeling chilly on a windy summit? Put one on.

Footgear. Alf Evers, the noted Catskill historian, quotes his son, Christopher: "They used to say that for six days the Lord labored at creating the Earth, and on the seventh he threw rocks at the Catskills." Rocky and stony trails are the rule in the Catskills, and require good-quality boots. Protection and comfort of the feet and ankles are essential to ensure an enjoyable hike. Enlist the help of a knowledgeable fitter to get a boot that is neither too tight nor too loose and that supports the ankle.

Generally, the steeper the trail or the heavier the climber, the more rugged the footwear needed. Take time to break in new boots. Work boots are sufficient for many hikes. Sneakers should be used only on flat and dry trails. As soon as a "hot spot" occurs (a blister can develop quickly), apply an ample circle of moleskin around the sore area. It works very well if applied in time. Some hikers wear an outer pair of woolen socks over a lighter pair of liner socks, both to reduce friction on long trips and for extra warmth on chilly days.

Food and water. Plan on drinking half a cup to a cup of water for every mile you hike. Don't underestimate the importance of water—and be sure to carry enough. The potability of backcountry water is not certain. Nausea, diarrhea, and vomiting can result from waterborne intestinal parasites such as Giardia lamblia and Cryptosporidium. Both iodine-based disinfectants, which work in 20 minutes, and portable water filters provide effective protection. As an alternative, water can be boiled for three minutes, if you carry a camp stove and fuel.

Suggestions for food include sandwiches, fruit, candy and granola bars, gorp (candy, raisins, nuts, sunflower seeds, granola, coconut, dried cereal), dried fruit, cookies, and food sticks. Eat small amounts at intervals rather then one large meal. Have a reserve supply in case of an emergency. A thermos to carry hot liquid like cocoa is a good investment.

First aid. Ideally, a minimum of three people are recommended for mountain or winter hiking. If there is an accident, one person can stay with the victim while

Leave No Trace

The Adirondack Mountain Club supports the seven principles of the Leave No Trace program:

1. Plan Ahead and Prepare
   - Know the regulations and special considerations for the area you'll visit
   - Prepare for extreme weather, hazards, and emergencies
   - Travel in groups of less than ten people to minimize impacts

2. Travel and Camp on Durable Surfaces
   - Hike in the middle of the trail; stay off of vegetation
   - Camp in designated sites where possible
   - In other areas, don't camp within 150 feet of water or a trail

3. Dispose of Waste Properly
   - Pack out all trash (including toilet paper), leftover food, and litter
   - Use existing privies, or dig a cat hole five to six inches deep, then cover hole
   - Wash yourself and dishes at least 150 feet from water

4. Leave What You Find
   - Leave rocks, plants, and other natural objects as you find them
   - Let photos, drawings, or journals help to capture your memories
   - Do not build structures or furniture or dig trenches

5. Minimize Campfire Impacts
   - Use a portable stove to avoid the lasting impact of a campfire
   - Where fires are permitted, use existing fire rings and only collect downed wood
   - Burn all fires to ash, put out campfires completely, then hide traces of fire

6. Respect Wildlife
   - Observe wildlife from a distance
   - Avoid wildlife during mating, nesting, and other sensitive times
   - Control pets at all times, and clean up after them

7. Be Considerate of Other Visitors
   - Respect other visitors and protect the quality of their experience
   - Let natural sounds prevail; avoid loud sounds and voices
   - Be courteous and yield to other users on the trail

For further information on Leave No Trace principles, log on to www.lnt.org.

the other seeks assistance.

Consider the following items to carry in a first-aid kit: ace bandage, moleskin, bandages, gauze pads, scissors, sunblock, safety pins, chapstick, antiseptic cream, and aspirin.

Equipment. The following are essential or recommended for a summer hike:

day pack	wool or fleece jacket or sweater
good boots	waterproof breathable shell or poncho
insect repellent	guidebook and map/compass
hat	flashlight with extra batteries
bandanna	waterproof matches
gloves	tissue or toilet paper, trowel*
water bottle(s)	water purification tablets
trail food	space blanket* *
jackknife	extra bag(s) for garbage
whistle	first-aid kit
extra socks	sunglasses
sunblock	candle * * *
camera	personal items
watch	small binoculars
moleskin	headnet in blackfly season

bread bags to wear over dry socks in the event of wet boots

trekking poles: increasingly used year-round when hiking in the mountains

* If there are no outhouses or bathrooms nearby, be prepared to dig a hole 5–6 inches deep, at least 150 ft from streams, and well off-trail. Cover with soil.
* * A lightweight, reflective sheet that can provide extra protection in emergencies because it reflects body heat back to the body.
* * * Facilitates fire starting in an emergency. Build your fire on a rock base, if possible. Use only dead or downed wood, and never leave a fire unattended. Douse thoroughly and cover with rocks. Note that fires above 3500 feet are only permitted in emergencies. Portable camp stoves are recommended for cooking. Some day-hikers carry stoves for emergencies.

It pays to "count your ounces" and avoid carrying unnecessary items. Go as light as is prudent.

Hunting season. Hiking during hunting season can be dangerous. Many hiking clubs do not schedule hikes during the regular hunting season. Big-game seasons in the Catskills are as follows:

• Regular season, deer: First Monday after November 15 through the first Tuesday after December 7.

• Regular season, bear: First Saturday of regular deer season through the first Tuesday after December 7.

• Archery season, deer and bear: October 15 through the day preceding regular deer season, and the five days following regular season.

If you do hike, wear bright clothing or the bright orange vests hunters often use.

Wildlife. The old forests were filled with panthers, wolves, bears, and bobcats. Now, perhaps the most hazardous creature is a porcupine. If you're hiking with an unleashed dog, it can get thoroughly pierced with quills. (Dogs should be leashed, at least when others approach, and droppings removed.) Porcupines are everywhere, and eat everything. If you hike all these trails, you'll see at least two downed airplanes thoroughly chewed by the critters, and numerous nibbled trail markers. We heard someone say that chicken wire is advised for cars, if you are heading off for an extended backpack. They chew brake lines. One climbed onto West Kill's lookout ledge with us as we were writing this book.

Black bears still live in the Catskills. They instinctively avoid people, but the behavior of a mother with cubs can be unpredictable. We once saw a mother bear with two cubs by a river. The cubs climbed a tree as the mother ran up the hill. If camping, remember that bears are omnivorous and are attracted by unprotected food and garbage. Never take any food into the tent with you. Unattended food also attracts smaller animals. Pack it securely.

Whitetail deer abound, especially near the many brooks and rivers. Coyotes or coydogs can be heard howling in the distance at twilight and during the night. Bobcat tracks meander through snow, though the animals themselves are seldom seen. Snowshoe hare tracks are all over the winter mountains. Mink, weasel, otter, beaver or their telltale signs are often observed. Most in evidence are the chirping chipmunks. Toads of many sizes and shades share the trail. Frogs and salamanders are fun to spot in ponds, lakes, and even permanent large puddles. Orange efts (formally called red efts, the land phase of a newt) are often found on the trail after a wet spell.

The abundant ruffed grouse startles you when it is startled, flapping through the trees. Wild turkey tracks are abundant, and occasionally you see the turkeys themselves, especially from your car. Hawks abound, and an occasional eagle searches for food above a brook. Bald eagles are nesting at New York City reservoirs like the Ashokan and Rondout. Ravens and vultures ride the thermals where land suddenly heaves up at the escarpment and in the cloves. Woodpeckers, and at night, owls make delightful sounds. You may catch a fleeting glimpse of a hummingbird, even on a mountain summit. Obtain field guides for the birds and plants of the northeast.

Snakes are uncommon and seldom of the poisonous variety. They are almost always harmless garter snakes. However, rattlesnakes have been seen on Overlook

Mountain and Mount Tremper. They try to avoid you. Other snakes are noted at Onteora Lake, in the Hudson River Valley.

Be aware that rabies has been spreading for several years. While it is most often associated with raccoons, any warm-blooded mammal can be a carrier. Avoid any wild animal that is behaving oddly. It is important that hikers do not pet or try to feed wild animals. If bitten by any animal, go immediately for medical care. Rabies is fatal if not treated right away.

Ticks spread Lyme disease, which can have the appearance of a rash spreading out from a large insect bite. Early detection is important. Prevention is best, by tucking pants bottoms into sock tops. As of this printing (2002), Lyme disease has been noted in Ulster County in the Catskills.

Blackflies are described in the Seasons section, under Spring.

Carry it in, carry it out. You will see this message on bulletin boards at trail-heads. Bring bread bags to carry litter, and consider picking up candy wrappers and other trash along the way. An interesting study shows that clean parks and outdoor areas tend to stay clean; pervasive litter breeds greater disorder. What we do and see affects others' behavior. It is depressing, indeed, to come across many bottles, cans, and paper products where people have enjoyed the wilderness, but have not left it nice for others. It is wonderful to come upon a pristine lean-to or campsite. Let's keep our beautiful trails and wilderness clean, for all to enjoy.

Hiking with Children

Hiking with any family member is a gift in this era of distractions, pressures, and structured activities. Hiking with children is a special gift. We have time on the trail to talk about many things, to share excitement and wonder, to learn from each other, to do spontaneous, unplanned things. Natural games develop, such as counting tiny toads or collecting stones and leaves. You might have a scavenger hunt for things typically found on the trail. The Catskills are full of interesting rocks with narrow crawl spaces between separated sections. Ask your companions about which animals might live in caves, rock crevices, and holes in trees and in the ground.

Youngsters want to do many things that adults don't think about and haven't planned. Discussing the hike in advance helps. Leave lots of extra time to let a child experience and explore the immediate surroundings. Look and have fun. This is an opportunity to be a fellow-adventurer. You might even bring a book to read while your child is enjoying nature's many offerings.

Keep in mind that children are closer to the ground! They like bugs, frogs, newts, pinecones, sticks, mud, and water. They are less interested in the sweeping vistas adults tend to appreciate. Children live in the moment, and so are not efficient or goal-oriented. The process is the important thing. They are endlessly curious about creatures and natural features we take for granted. Let them open our eyes again.

Like all of us, children may hit energy lows or get into negative frames of mind. Keep great snacks on hand and offer plenty of fluids, for children need to drink more than we do. Thirst is not a good indicator of fluid requirements. At a minimum, stop every hour for fluids.

Many children like to carry their own small pack or fanny-pack for juice or water and snacks. They might bring a magnifying glass, compass, and flashlight. Keep the pace suitable for the slowest member of the group. As much as possible, encourage and suggest, but don't force, ideas of your own. If the children need a diversion, a member of the group might go ahead a bit and hide a favorite toy or interesting object for them to seek.

Often, hiking with friends increases the fun and energy levels. Use the buddy system. A good idea is to tell your child never to pass a sign or junction without waiting for you, if he or she runs ahead. Encourage them to be aware of staying on the trail and getting back to the trail if exploring off-trail. Stay within calling distance, although in the woods that is surprisingly close. Have each hiker carry a whistle, and if separated from the group, stay in one place while blowing the whistle. Tell children that the chance of getting lost is greatest on descents, because paths no longer converge on one spot.

Stress taking care on rocks, which are slippery in the Catskills, especially on the descent, and that wet roots and logs are also very slippery. Carry young children in dangerous areas or avoid areas with sharp drops.

Keep trips short. By age five or six, children can handle moderate trips, although every child is different both physically and emotionally. By age nine, ability to sustain rigorous activity develops. Plan a hike as part of a trip that offers other activities. Reminisce about the fun aspects of a hike to build good memories of being together outdoors. You will learn what to repeat or omit so they are more likely to want to go again. Recording hikes and memories builds a sense of accomplishment. Leave extra food and drinks in the car, and extra clothing for a dry ride home.

These suggestions will leave a child eager for more. For greater detail and additional ideas, you may wish to consult Before You Lace Up, the first chapter of *Kids on the Trail! Hiking with Children in the Adirondacks,* by Rose Rivezzi and David Trithart. Although the trail information is Adirondack-specific, the authors' advice and information has broad applicability.

The Seasons

Spring. One of Mother Nature's mischievous tricks is the blackfly, which comes out just as you want to come out and enjoy the profusion of trilliums, hepatica, violets, trout lilies, spring beauties, Dutchman's-breeches, and mountain laurel. The blackfly is a small, gnat-like, biting insect that hatches only in cold mountain streams. It is not generally found elsewhere than in the mountains, because it doesn't breed in standing water or lakes. You may not be familiar with this pesky phenomenon.

Conventional wisdom has it that blackfly season extends from Mother's Day to Father's Day, but it often lasts to July. The bite is similar to a mosquito bite, itchy for several days. Bug repellents are minimally effective against the blackfly and do nothing to deter their persistent hovering about your face and hair. Clouds of blackflies surround you if you are still or moving slowly. Long sleeves and pants are recommended during blackfly season, for unlike mosquitoes, the blackfly cannot bite through fabric. Hats are helpful, and head nets are available to protect the neck, ear, and hairline area that they seem to relish.

We recommend planning long treks or slow-paced climbs for later summer or fall. If your outings will be on the level, and you can keep up a brisk pace, the blackfly impact will be minimal, for unlike mosquitoes they do not aggressively pursue you, but do bite if you're still. The pesky critters make sitting and enjoying the sights during breaks less enjoyable.

Springtime usually brings muddier trails, so wear hiking boots and gaiters. Snowmelt and frequent rain can make brook crossings difficult, where no bridge is provided. Read through an entire hike description, so you will know which hikes have potentially high brooks.

Ice and snow can still cling to the higher mountains, particularly on the northern slopes, until late spring. On high-traffic peaks, the trails are broken nearly all year long, but deep snow may be present until May on less-used high trails, requiring snowshoes and gaiters. Be wary of "black ice" ledges which still have thin and not easily spotted ice. South-facing trails are much drier.

Summer. By midsummer, the hot, dry weather ends the worst of the blackfly problem. Mosquitoes still linger around ponds, lakes, and marshy areas, so read through the hikes and pick treks that avoid those areas until later. By midsummer mosquitoes are usually no problem on a mountain climb, but bring repellent. Dark colors attract mosquitoes.

Don't leave a backpack unattended for any extended period if it has food in it. Although bear encounters are very rare and bears seek to avoid humans, they are attracted by food of all kinds. (Never bring food into a tent, and hang food in bear bags if no car is nearby.)

Consider wearing synthetic or cotton blend fabrics, because they dry much faster than 100 percent cotton clothing. Summits are often very windy and noticeably cooler, and you can become chilled in wet fabric. Bring an extra top to change into, and pack a sweater or jacket. Especially when hiking with children, it is important to remember that hypothermia occurs most often between thirty and fifty degrees Fahrenheit and that summit wind-chill can bring a summer hike into this temperature range. Mountain weather changes rapidly, and what starts as a warm, sunny day can become cloudy, windy, or stormy. Check weather reports and bring rain gear.

July and August bring berry season, and many mountain areas are covered with raspberry, blackberry, and blueberry bushes. You may want to bring a container to collect berries.

Autumn. This is the best season for hiking, according to many. The air is cooler and drier, the scenery is spectacular, and most of the bugs are gone. By October, the leaves are off the trees at higher elevations, making many hikes a great deal more rewarding. Certain summit viewpoints are partially obscured by trees in summer, but now, with the leaves falling, the vistas are much improved. Throughout the hike, surrounding mountains can be seen.

Refer to the hunting season section in Before You Go, above. It is important to stop venturing into the woods during this period. If you do hike, wear bright clothing, keep to marked trails, and exercise caution.

Winter. Full crampons and snowshoes should be worn or carried on winter hikes. Conditions in the upper reaches of a mountain are likely to be different from those at the trailhead. The Catskill's delightful ledges are often icy and can be treacherous; crampons can help maintain a firm footing. Ski poles or trekking poles are essential. The characteristic narrow cloves and notches in this region mean that many ascents are steep, especially in the Devils Path section. Therefore, it is important to note the day's snow conditions before setting off. For example, if a thaw is followed by a freeze, snow can become hard-glazed. Without crampons, secure footing is difficult on such a surface on steep terrain. Practice using new crampons and snowshoes on easy terrain.

Know the weather forecast and choose days with minimal wind to hike and climb in winter. If you're hiking on a twenty-degree day (minus seven degrees Celsius), with the wind a moderate breeze of fifteen mph, the wind chill is minus five degrees Fahrenheit (minus twenty degrees Celsius). Another three to five degrees Fahrenheit (two to three degrees Celsius) is lost for each thousand feet of ascent. Protection from the wind is as important as insulation from the cold. Frostbite is the freezing of body tissue. It can happen quickly in windy, cold conditions. Do not expose extremities for any length of time, and change into dry socks covered with plastic bags in the event you break through ice. Remember also that weather can change quickly in any season, especially in mountainous areas.

Winter hiking on sunny, windless days can be hot. You may hike in one layer and add three more layers on a summit. Carry or wear several layers of appropriate clothing. Ideal layering for winter hiking is:

- Capilene or polypropylene long underwear. Active outdoor sports require underwear that is warm and comfortable, yet allows perspiration and body heat to escape to outer layers.
- Synthetic fleece, like polarfleece, or wool shirt/sweater and pants, for the second layer.
- Down vest or jacket for additional warmth, but remember that down becomes useless when wet. Pack down garments in a plastic bag.
- Gore-Tex jacket and pants, for relatively breathable and waterproof wind protection.

Cotton fabric is poor for mountain hiking. (See Before You Go earlier in this section for more detail.)

Carry at least two pairs of mittens, as they are warmer than gloves. Liner gloves are good to allow dexterity, such as for tying snowshoes, without baring extremities. Worn inside mittens, they are more easily washed and add a bit of extra warmth. Over-mitts keep hands drier. Up to fifty percent of body heat loss is through the head and neck. Carry a maximum-warmth hat or balaclava for inactive periods; neck-warmers are available, also. An ear-warmer without hat allows more heat to escape when active. Many types of boots are available to keep the feet warm and relatively dry, and the ankles protected. Good hiking socks and/or wool socks, plus gaiters, complete the clothing requirements. Remember that your clothing should be adequate for periods of inactivity (eating lunch or in case of injury), and that the body cools down quickly on a windy mountain.

Start early, for daylight hours are short. Calculate the extra time needed to break trail in deep snow conditions. Always carry extra batteries and flashlights, preferably headlamps, to keep your arms free to use ski poles. Your vehicle should be in good operating condition and have plenty of gas. Many trailheads are at the end of long, isolated roads. Carry a shovel, sleeping bags, and extra food and water in the car. Consider carrying a lightweight but warm sleeping bag on your pack for long winter outings, so you will have protection in case of injury.

Catskill Day Hikes is not a complete guide for winter hiking. ADK's *Winterwise: A Backpacker's Guide* by John Dunn is a good resource. It's best to start winter hiking in the company of experienced outdoorspeople such as members of the Adirondack Mountain Club or the Catskill 3500 Club. Both organizations can provide guidance and year-round hiking schedules.

The Catskills

Tectonic collisions first formed the Adirondacks one billion years ago. Five hundred million years ago, a series of collisions formed the Appalachians, and the Taconic mountains rose to the east. A sea formed where the Catskills are now. Eight thousand feet of sediments accumulated, forming the characteristic sedimentary shales, bluestones, and red and green shales of the northeast Catskills. A final collision created the mountains of New England and caused the uprising of the large Catskill Delta, including the Pocono area.

In the millennia since, erosion has gouged out the steep cloves and notches of the Catskills. Glacial meltwaters formed the many waterfalls in the region, but the shales and sandstones absorbed water and created underground aquifers instead of the lakes characteristic of the granite Adirondacks.

Though geologists tell us that the Catskills are the eroded edge of the Allegheny Plateau and only *appear* to be mountains, this book uses the convention that if it looks like a mountain, and it hikes like a mountain, it's a mountain! The hiker notices the difference between the Adirondacks and the Catskills not so much in the rigor, but in the terrain. The Catskill hiker starts in a narrow clove and climbs steeply upward to a flat summit, whereas the Adirondack hiker has moderate beginning grades and ends on a definite summit. Catskill trails are drier and less muddy, and the rocks are slippery on wet slopes, whereas in the Adirondacks you can trust your boots to cling to the granite more reliably.

Early settlers in the region avoided the forbidding forests behind what had come to be known locally as the Great Wall of Manitou, which rises 1600 feet above the Hudson River Valley. The various Native American peoples did most of their hunting and farming in the river valleys. The colonists' fear of these dark, hemlock-covered mountains was reflected in the names they bestowed: the Devils Kitchen, Devils Path, Hell Falls, Devils Tombstone.

By the early nineteenth century, the abundant hemlock was providing tannin for dozens of tanneries in the region. Leather for saddles and harnesses was big business in the era preceding trains and cars. Finished leather was transported over rocky roads to the Hudson port of Saugerties to be shipped worldwide. In one year, 6,000 cords of hemlock bark provided tannin for working 60,000 hides at one tannery. Entire groves of old-growth hemlock disappeared, altering the forest with the growth of birch, oak, and maple. The thousands of feet of sedimentary rock created a second major industry, quarrying the attractive blue-gray slate called bluestone, which paved many streets and parks of cities here and abroad.

It wasn't until the mountains were discovered as a recreational and inspirational retreat from hot, polluted urban areas that people in large numbers began coming to the Catskills. Steamboats and railroads brought the wealthy and famous from New York, Washington, and other cities to the grand new hotels built on top of the Great Wall of Manitou. The art of the Hudson River School of landscape painting, Washington Irving's legendary "Rip Van Winkle," and John Burroughs's nature writings further introduced this beautiful region to poets, writers, artists, and all those fortunate enough to make the excursion to what was becoming a world-famous area.

During the late nineteenth century, one of the earliest attempts at land preservation took place in Albany. In 1885, legislation was passed that established the Forest Preserve, and directed that the public lands in the Adirondack and Catskill regions, "be forever kept as wild forest lands." Article XIV of the New York State Constitution mandates that the Forest Preserve lands "shall not be leased, sold or exchanged, or be taken by any corporation, public or private, nor shall the timber thereon be sold, removed or destroyed." New York is the only state where such constitutional protection has been granted by the citizens.

The Catskill Park was created in 1904. Its boundary encompasses 700,000 acres of public and private land in Greene, Sullivan, Ulster, and Delaware Counties. Over the last 100 years, the state of New York has acquired nearly 300,000 acres within the Park. These public lands constitute the Catskill portion of the New York State Forest Preserve. The Catskill Park State Land Master Plan was released by the DEC in 1985. New trails are continually being created.

Most hikes in this book are within the Park "blue line" boundary, roughly bounded by NY 23 to the north, NY 30 to the west, north of NY 17 and NY 55 to the south, and skirting the Ashokan Reservoir to NY 32 on the east.

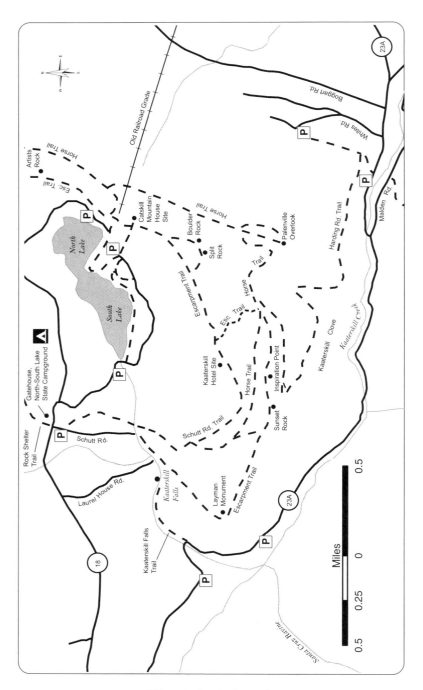

Hikes 1, 2, 6, 7, and 8

"The longer I live, the more I am impressed

with the beauty and wonder of the world."

—JOHN BURROUGHS

Northeast Catskills: North-South Lake and Palenville Area

This region of shimmering lakes, exquisite waterfalls, precipitous cliffs, and mountain vistas established the Catskills as one of the world's major vacation destinations in the nineteenth century. The long-held idea of nature as alien and dangerous was transformed by the works of the Hudson River School of landscape painting, and by the writings of naturalists and local spinners of lore, into appreciation of the pristine waters, forests, and mountains as places of rugged beauty where one might renew oneself spiritually and physically.

Great hotels were created on the very edge of the Great Wall of Manitou. Disembarking from Hudson River steamboats, the rich and famous boarded the trains of a narrow-gauge railroad to Palenville. There stagecoaches brought them up the escarpment on newly created roadways, marvels of engineering wizardry for that era. Modern trails of the North Lake area evolved from those roads and from other routes that connected great hotels like Catskill Mountain House and Hotel Kaaterskill. Another narrow-gauge railroad was created by blasting through narrow Stony Clove from Phoenicia to Hunter, then over to South Lake. Soon a 1630-foot cable funicular railroad was constructed straight up the Great Wall of Manitou.

In the popular North-South Lake area, the southern section of the 23-mile Escarpment Trail was begun in 1932 by A.T. Shorey, who later created Adirondack trails as well. This is one of the most spectacular trails in the Catskills, with many cliff-edge vistas. The North-South Lake state campground is a fine base from which to explore the trails we describe in this section.

Hikes in the North-South Lake area often involve little or no difference in overall elevation between starting and ending points, although the trail is likely to include ascents and descents. Thus the summary information with each description only occasionally notes an elevation change. Also, because there are no true summits, high points are noted where these pertain.

If you have time after a hike or want a change of pace, consider one of the following local attractions:

Lake Rip Van Winkle. From NY 23A in Tannersville, turn south on Depot Street. Supervised swimming, picnicking, facilities.

Mountaintop Arboretum. Free public 10-acre preserve of botanically identified flowering trees and shrubs from many areas of the world. Woodland walk, guided tours, newsletter, and educational programs. From NY 23A, travel north from Tannersville for 2 mi on County Route 23C. 518-589-3903.

Colgate Lake. Unsupervised swimming, fishing, boating (no motors or electric). Travel north on County Route 23C from Tannersville to East Jewett, turning east on County Route 78 for 1.6 mi. Colgate Lake Trail to the Escarpment Trail is another 0.1 mi.

Hunter Lake. From NY 23A in Hunter, turn towards Hunter Mountain Ski Bowl, then turn left onto Ski Bowl Road. Supervised swimming, picnic tables, facilities. See Devil's Path section for nearby hikes.

Hunter Mountain Ski Museum. Skiing antiques from 1700. Open all year. Main Lodge, Hunter Mountain Ski Bowl, NY 23A, Hunter, NY. 888-HunterMtn.

Sky Ride, Hunter Mountain Colonels Chair. Ride a ski lift from Hunter Mountain Ski Bowl Main Lodge to Summit Lodge. Saturdays and Sundays from first weekend in July to Columbus Day. 10 A.M.–5 P.M. 888-HunterMtn. 518-263-4223.

Devil's Tombstone and Notch Lake at Devil's Tombstone Public Campground. The Devil's Tombstone is a great boulder now adorned with the centennial plaque commemorating the one hundredth anniversary of the establishment of New York State's "forever wild" Forest Preserve. The Preserve is protected by the Constitution of New York State. Notch Lake is 0.2 mi north, with a seasonal parking fee payable at camp office. This location is for picnicking, not swimming.

North-South Lake. From NY 23A in Haines Falls, turn north on County Route 18, where a DEC sign indicates North-South Lake state campground. Bear right after one block and travel 2.3 mi to the gatehouse. Beaches are offered at both lakes, and nonmotorized boats are available for rent. See North-South Lake section for many hikes.

1. Inspiration Point and Hudson River Valley Lookout

Round-trip distance: 3.8 mi (6.1 km); longer loop, 5.1 mi (8.2 km)
Elevation change: 150 ft (46 m)
High-point elevation: Inspiration Point, 2000 ft (610 m)
Difficulty: Moderately easy
Maps: Page 30; Trail Conference Map 40 (P-3); USGS Kaaterskill 7.5'

Summary: A spectacular hike in the North-South Lake area of the northeastern Catskills, along the southern Escarpment Trail 1000 ft above Kaaterskill Clove. Vistas abound, west to Hunter Mountain ski trails, across the drop to Kaaterskill High Peak and Roundtop Mountain, and east to the Hudson River Valley. From lookout ledges and narrow sections of trail, drops of hundreds of feet require caution, especially with children. Connecting trails offer many possibilities for extending a hike or for superb views on short treks.

Access to area: From the east, take NY 23A to Palenville and up Kaaterskill Clove to County Route 18 (North Lake Road), turning north at the North-South Lake state campground sign. From the west on NY 23A in Haines Falls, turn north on County Route 18 at the campground sign. Bear right after one block. Travel 2.2 mi and turn right on Schutt Road, just before the entrance to North-South Lake state campground.

Parking and trailhead: The large DEC parking area is on the right, 200 ft down Schutt Road. The blue-marked Escarpment Trail is directly across the road.

The first 0.5 mi parallels Schutt Road. Owing to its use as a horse trail, the ground is eroded and can be muddy in wet weather. (You can walk down Schutt Road instead. At its end, follow a path on the left, along the creek to a nearby bridge and turn right on the blue-marked Escarpment Trail.)

If you hike via the trail, you will pass through a large stone wall and cross an old railroad bed, signs of the bygone era when splendid hotels and their connecting railroads attracted tourists from near and far.

After crossing two bridges, turn right at the junction down a stony lane, passing a barrier. Bear left into the woods, continuing on the blue-marked trail. The trek through the pretty woods leads to a steep 200-foot descent to Layman Monument, which recognizes Frank Layman, who lost his life here fighting a forest fire in 1900. A short climb leads to an open ledge with excellent views across Kaaterskill Clove to homes that seem about to fall into the gorge below.

The trail passes between walls of layered rock that built up through millennia of sediment deposits when the Catskill area was under the sea. From here, the trail regains the 200 ft it descended to the monument.

Note the junction with a yellow-marked trail, because this is one of your possible return routes. Enjoy the now-level trek near the edge of the escarpment. Breezes blow up through the clove and great rock ledges jut out. Be careful of loose stones on a sloping lookout ledge called Sunset Rock.

Continue to the much larger ledges and better views from Inspiration Point, just a short distance down enormous conglomerate boulders. You're standing at 2000 ft, 1200 ft above Kaaterskill Creek. About 0.1 mi farther is a spot that offers different views, east to the Hudson River Valley. Sit on a ledge and enjoy the ravens and vultures riding the thermals.

If you retrace your route from here, the total return is 1.6 mi. At the junction you passed, turn right on the yellow-marked trail and continue, passing a horse trail on right, to the red-marked Schutt Road Trail. Turn left to the original blue-marked trail, crossing the bridge and ascending gradually back to the parking area.

If you continue along the escarpment from the Hudson River Valley view, the return loop is 2.9 mi. Special features on this route include passing next to a cliff at the trail's edge (keep children in tow), and bounteous mountain laurel that bloom in June. Beyond the cliff, the trail moves away from the escarpment edge and its lookouts.

If you choose this longer loop, continue on the Escarpment Trail to a second junction, turning left to continue on the blue-marked trail. After ascending 200 ft in 0.6 mi, turn left on the red-marked Schutt Road Trail to the original blue-marked trail, crossing the bridge for the final trek to the parking area.

2. Boulder Rock and Split Rock Loop

Round-trip distance: 1.5 mi (2.4 km); with loop, 1.8 mi (2.9 km)
Elevation change: 200 ft (61 m)
High-point elevation: Boulder Rock, 2400 ft (732 m)
Difficulty: Moderately easy. Short; easy to former Catskill Mountain House
    overlook; short, steep ascents to Boulder Rock
Maps: Page 30; Trail Conference Map 40 (P-3); USGS Kaaterskill 7.5'

Summary: Visit the site of the Catskill Mountain House with its sweeping views of the Hudson River Valley. Imagine this grand hotel, one of America's first and finest resorts, with its thirteen Corinthian columns and 315 rooms.

Then hike the Escarpment Trail up the shoulder of South Mountain to one of the fine vistas from the escarpment wall. Before you lies an immense area of eastern New York State.

▶ **Access to area**:   From the east, take NY 23A to Palenville and up Kaaterskill Clove. In Haines Falls, turn north on County Route 18 (North Lake Road) at a large brown and yellow sign for North-South Lake state campground. From the west on NY 23A, turn north on County Route 18 in Haines Falls. Bear right after one block and travel 2.3 mi to the campground. Past the gatehouse, take the right fork to South Lake. Pass the large parking area for the beach and bear right to the last parking area.

The North-South Lake state campground is closed from late October to early May. (Call 800-456-CAMP for exact dates and fee information.) When the campground is closed, turn right after the gatehouse and drive to the parking area at the west end of South Lake. Walk 0.8 mi on the road, or hike the yellow-marked trail beginning beyond the guardrail. Follow the road to the last parking area, bearing right at a fork to a pavilion. Cross to the Catskill Mountain House sign.

If you hike the trail along South Lake, turn right to the road when you emerge at the beach and follow the above directions.

Parking and trailhead: Park at the far end of the parking area where the sign points the way to Catskill Mountain House. The broad path leaves the northeast corner of the parking area. ◀

The trail heads east for one-quarter mile to the site of the Catskill Mountain House, a breathtaking spot overlooking the Hudson River Valley at the very edge of the escarpment. Take a few moments to read the exhibits about the famous Catskill Mountain House, the destination of presidents and world travelers. A cable funicular railroad climbed the escarpment to bring seekers of beauty to these lakes and views. At night, boats on the Hudson River focused their spotlights on the famous hotel.

Head south on the blue-marked Escarpment Trail, to the right of the exhibit boards. Take your time ascending the steep side of South Mountain, and enjoy the rock overhangs above the trail register. You will soon finish the steep climb, and see that it is well worth the effort. All along the way, white and pink mountain laurel bloom in late June. On a sunny day, the scent of pine fills the air.

The trail reaches an enormous conglomerate rock outcrop, above which is a lovely area reminiscent of a planned rock garden. Here the trail is level, with pine needles and flat rock. A great sloped boulder with "graffiti" from the 1850s invites climbing. (This is not Boulder Rock.) There is a lookout ledge to the east, beyond. The trail ascends a different type of rock, the characteristic rippled and layered sedimentary rock of the Catskills. Note the "peeling paint" fungus.

When you reach a junction, do not take the red-marked cutoff trail to the right, which bypasses Boulder Rock and Split Rock. You will return via this cutoff later. Continue left another 0.1 mi on the blue-marked trail, a short, steep pitch down toward Boulder Rock.

At 0.5 mi, as you walk through blueberry bushes, you can see huge Boulder Rock ahead, and are treated to fine views to the east and south from the large, open ledge. **Caution;** the terrain drops precipitously! You are standing 1800 ft above Palenville. Kaaterskill High Peak rises out of the valley near to the south.

Continue past the boulder to Split Rock just beyond. Split Rock might alarm someone afraid of heights, for you walk a narrow trail right next to drop-offs of several dozen feet. Be especially cautious if the terrain is wet; rock in the Catskills is more slippery than the granite of the Adirondacks. You feel like you're in "Honey, I shrunk the kids" territory, next to enormous blocks of rock that have split off the hillside. You pass a balanced rock in the woods after Split Rock.

Continue to the junction and turn right on the red-marked cutoff trail. This loop is very pretty, passing through large mountain laurel adorning the trail. You are looping back to the junction for the trail to Boulder Rock; bear left to return to the Catskill Mountain House area, then follow the broad path, left, back to the parking area.

3. Sunset Rock and Newmans Ledge

Round-trip distance: Sunset Rock, 2.3 mi (3.7 km);
   Newmans Ledge, 2.7 mi (4.4 km)
Elevation change: 400 ft (122 m)
High-point elevation: Sunset Rock, 2350 ft (717 m);
   Newmans Ledge, 2500 ft (762 m)
Difficulty: Moderately easy, but several steep scrambles
Maps: Page 40; Trail Conference Map 40 (P-3); USGS Kaaterskill 7.5'

Summary: This trail from the North Lake beach area follows dramatic rock outcrops and lovely woods to an extensive open rock zone that is cleaved with deep crevices that require careful exploring. This is a magnificent spot to have lunch, with expansive views of the lakes and mountains. The vista over the Hudson River Valley is spectacular at Artists Rock along the way to Sunset Rock, and at Newmans Ledge. Drops of hundreds of feet in several places require caution, especially with children.

▶ **Access to area:** From the east, take NY 23A to Palenville and up Kaaterskill Clove to County Route 18 (North Lake Road). Look for a sign for the North-South Lake state campground. From the west on NY 23A in Haines Falls, turn north on County Route 18 (look for campground sign). Bear right after one block, and travel 2.3 mi to the gatehouse. Bear left beyond it and travel to the North Lake parking area.

The North-South Lake state campground is closed from late October to early May. (Call 800-456-CAMP for exact dates and fee information.) When the campground is closed, turn right after the gatehouse and drive to the parking area at the west end of South Lake. Walk 0.8 mi on the road, or hike the yellow-marked trail beyond the guardrail. Follow the road to the last parking area, bearing right at a fork to a pavilion. Cross to the Catskill Mountain House sign and follow the path to the next sign, "Historic Site, Catskill Mountain House."

Turn left here, following the blue-marked Escarpment Trail down a scenic old road with large, mossy ledges. Pass the barrier, and at a DEC sign for "Artists Rock," continue across the open area (not right) to a path down a gulley, which is the unmarked Escarpment Trail. Upon reaching a fence, continue straight ahead along the fence (not on the path descending to the right). Continue on the blue-marked trail.

Parking and trailhead: There is a picnic area across the parking lot from the bathhouse. Go past the picnic tables to the high wire fence. Turn left on the blue-marked Escarpment Trail. ◀

Continue past the picnic area into pine and hemlock woods, walking on flat rock to a dramatic drop many feet down to your right. This is a lovely area where mountain laurel bloom in late June. A slight ascent brings you to the trail register. You soon reach a large pitch upward, which becomes an all-body workout as you scramble up the ledges and boulders. Take care here, especially as you descend on your return.

Above, the trail levels out along an interesting section of extensive flat rock and pitch pine. It then goes right over to the escarpment edge, hundreds of feet straight down. The trail turns left at the rock ledge favored by Thomas Cole and other artists of the Hudson River School. Called Artists Rock, this beauty spot affords unbeatable views east over the Hudson River Valley. You can see the straight expanse of Rip Van Winkle Bridge at the city of Catskill. Roundtop Mountain may be seen beyond the ridge above the Sleepy Hollow Trail where Rips Rock juts out.

A brief climb up the hillside levels into a scenic stroll through park-like woods. After scaling one large ledge, you reach the base of the great conglomerate rock bluff, on top of which is your destination. Its steepness requires climbing around the base of this interesting area, sometimes underneath large overhangs. Picture all this rock at the bottom of an ancient sea!

At a junction, turn right on the yellow-marked spur trail. This is a short, pretty trek (not 0.3 mi as the sign says, but 0.2 mi) through terrain reminiscent of a cultivated rock garden, with long-needled pines, pink and white mountain laurel and pleasant walking on flat rock. Views east to the Hudson River Valley begin. Soon, where a large boulder is perched on the trail, turn right toward the extensive, open ledges called Sunset Rock. (If you follow yellow markers, when you arrive at a precipice, turn right and you'll see an obscured yellow marker. Sunset Rock is just beyond.)

This is one of the magical places in the Catskills. Magnificent views open to the south and west, with North-South Lake shimmering below. With binoculars, you can see a picnic table on one of the islands. Kaaterskill High Peak and Roundtop Mountain dominate the skyline like great breaking waves. Devils Path peaks, Plateau Mountain and Hunter Mountain, appear farther west. Far to the south, the craggy Shawangunks are visible on the horizon. Very deep crevices on Sunset Rock require care while exploring.

When you can tear yourself away, retrace your steps on the spur trail to the blue-marked Escarpment Trail junction, and turn right to Newmans Ledge, another 0.2 mi. You ascend steeply, then walk along the edge of the cliff you just ascended. Newmans Ledge offers sweeping views east and north. On clear days you can see beyond Albany. You feel as if you're on the edge of the world here. Ravens glide in the breezes rising up the escarpment. You are 1900 ft above Palenville.

(If you wish to continue this adventure, you can hike up to North Point. See "North Point Loop" hike for what to expect. You could return from North Point via Marys Glen (the loop ascent route), making the hike a mile shorter than retracing via Newmans Ledge and Sunset Rock.)

4. North Point Loop

Round-trip distance: 4.7 mi (7.6 km)
Elevation change: 740 ft (226 m)
Summit Elevation: 2940 ft (896 m)
Difficulty: Moderate. Near-vertical scramble onto North Point,
    steep pitches throughout loop.
Maps: Page 40; Trail Conference Map 40 (P-3); USGS Kaaterskill 7.5'

Summary: The hiker to beautiful North Point will be rewarded with magnificent vistas, looking far down to North-South Lake, south and west to Kaaterskill High Peak, Roundtop, Hunter, and Plateau Mountains, and east across the Hudson River Valley. Large, open rock ledges invite an extended stay, soaking up the sun and enjoying lunch with a view. Explore around the rock edge east and north to more fine views of the Blackhead Range and Windham High Peak far beyond. Pick a very clear day to see forever at this truly spectacular place.

▶ **Access to area:**   From the east, take NY 23A to Palenville and up Kaaterskill Clove to County Route 18 (North Lake Road). Look for a sign for North-South Lake state campground. From the west on NY 23A in Haines Falls, turn north on County Route 18 (look for campground sign). Bear right after one block and travel 2.3 mi to the gatehouse. Bear left beyond it, and travel 0.9 mi to Marys Glen Trail on the left.

The North-South Lake state campground is closed from late October to early May. (Call 800-456-CAMP for exact dates and fee information.) When the campground is closed, North Point is best accessed via the yellow-marked Rock Shelter Trail across from Schutt Road just before the gatehouse. In 1.3 mi, turn left on red-marked Marys Glen Trail and follow the directions below. Returning, turn right on Marys Glen Trail at the first junction, then right again on the Rock Shelter Trail at the second junction.

Parking and trailhead: The parking area is on the left a short distance beyond the trailhead. ◀

Follow the red-marked trail north along the west side of Ashley Creek. The primary water source of North Lake, it once provided water for the Catskill Mountain House. We were told by a long-time Hunter resident that the lakes were artificially created, and ice was harvested for the iceboxes of the great hotels.

This part of Marys Glen Trail is very rocky and tree roots are exposed due to heavy use, but soon the rock becomes flatter and easier to traverse. Turn right at a junction along a yellow-marked short spur path to Ashley Falls. Although it can be dry, the falls area is a very impressive place, with enormous rock slabs and ledges. Returning, continue steeply up the trail to the top of the falls, where the trail crosses the stream into a pretty hemlock and birch woods. Mostly on flat rocks and ledges, the trail passes a junction with the yellow-marked Rock Shelter Trail on the right, then a dramatic high ledge and a second junction, left. Continue on the red trail.

The trail ascends interesting rock ledges, then winds through level sections of deciduous woods. Patches of coal begin appearing on the path. Note a clearing back in a hemlock woods, right, where you can find remnants of a cast-iron stove strewn through the mossy understory. The Marys Glen Trail

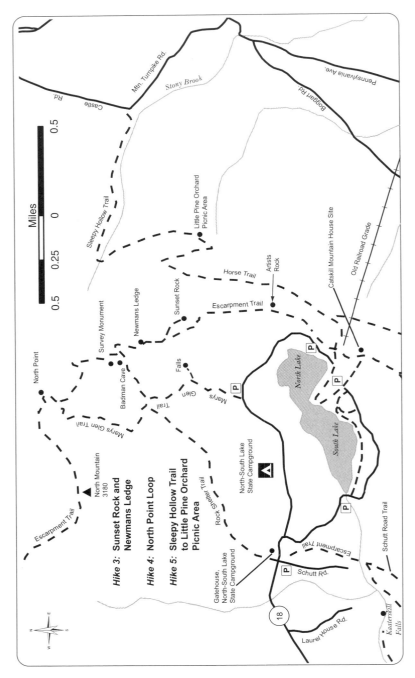

Hikes 3, 4, and 5

ends at a third junction. Continue left on the blue-marked Escarpment Trail soon swinging left up the rocky hillside, which can obscure the trail. After steeply ascending a cliff, you come to an open rock ledge with beautiful views of North-South Lake and Kaaterskill High Peak, a great spot for a break.

After brief, moderate climbing, huge rock outcrops appear ahead, and a fun (some may say challenging) scramble awaits—straight up the rock. The North Point overlook has one of the Catskill's finest views of lakes, valleys, and mountains, with plenty of room to spread out on its various ledges high above the forest you've just traveled. Be sure to follow the rock edge east and north to other great vistas as far as the Blackhead Range and Windham High Peak. Albany is visible on a clear day.

After you've soaked up the sun and the views at North Point, be sure to continue exploring up the Escarpment Trail past Moon Rock Shelter, a rock overhang, to Moon Rock. Go a bit farther to another open area with views down to North Point. Retrace your steps from here.

When you reach the first junction on the descent, turn left, staying on the blue-marked Escarpment Trail to begin a different return. Along the escarpment, the vegetation changes to mountain laurel and blueberries. The trail becomes a delightful walk on soft pine needles and flat rock through shady spruce, hemlock, and long-needled pine groves. You suddenly emerge onto a large open meadow of flat rock and blueberry bushes, with good views southwest to Kaaterskill High Peak and Roundtop Mountain.

Descending large rocky ledges and wonderful outcrops, you arrive at Badman Cave, an irresistible spot to scramble around. Legend has it that outlaws lived here in the eighteenth century. At the junction just below, bear left to the spectacular views from Newmans Ledge, Sunset Rock, and Artists Rock described in Hike 3. You will pass rock outcrops off the trail on the left with narrow passages to walk through. Alternating steep and level sections bring you to awesome views of the Hudson River Valley from Newmans Ledge. Walk along the cliff top 0.2 mi to the scramble down to the Sunset Rock junction. (Take the short yellow spur trail to Sunset Rock, if you haven't yet visited this magnificent spot. See Hike 3.)

Follow the blue-marked Escarpment Trail, passing Artists Rock, to the trail register. Look for paths heading right a short distance to the campground road. At the road, turn right. Marys Glen parking area is a 10–15 minute walk.

5. Sleepy Hollow Trail to Little Pine Orchard Picnic Area

Round-trip distance: 3.0 mi (4.8 km)
Elevation change: 800 ft (244 m)
High-point elevation: 1500 ft (457 m)
Difficulty: Moderate
Maps: Page 40; Trail Conference Map 41 (P-3); USGS Kaaterskill 7.5'

Summary: Ascend 800 ft and over one hundred years into historic Sleepy Hollow on a broad old lane to a picnic area with beautiful views of the Hudson River Valley.

▶ **Access to area:** In Palenville, traveling west on NY 23A, turn north on Boggart Road. The Horse Trail parking area is on the left in 2.1 mi, but continue to the hiker trailhead, bearing left at the Pennsylvania Avenue junction and continuing to Mountain Turnpike Road at 2.4 mi. Turn left here for 0.8 mi.

Parking and trailhead: Do not use the private home parking area at the road's end, but park down along the wide shoulder of the road. The trail begins at the end of pavement.◀

The Sleepy Hollow Trail, part of the historic Little Delaware Turnpike, heads up Rip Van Winkle Hollow (Sleepy Hollow) above the cascading Rip Van Winkle Brook.

This trail, now sometimes called the Mountain House Road, is a broad trail into the narrowing hollow. The atmosphere created by the dark hemlock gave rise to legends of the fearsome land on "The Great Wall of Manitou" that rises 1600 ft out of the Hudson River Valley to the mountains. Native American stories and legends brought from Europe combined with rich local imaginations about wildcats and evil spirits populating this unexplored region. It wasn't long before industry, tourism, art, and literature transformed this area into one of the most sought-after spots in the new world.

Crossing tiny Black Snake Bridge at 0.5 mi, the lane switchbacks to the southeast at 1.0 mi, near the trail register. Just beyond on the right is the site of the Rip Van Winkle House, an old inn along this legendary road to the Catskill Mountain House. We found an 1881 penny near its foundation. Legend has it that Rip Van Winkle slept near here those twenty long years on Rips Boulder. (Six hundred feet above it is a cliff known as Rips Rock.) Stagecoaches brought tourists seeking refuge from the summer heat up this steep 1600-foot escarpment. Two more horses were needed for a stage's steep ascent of Dead Ox Hill. Passengers often had to get out and walk. In 1882, a narrow-gauge railroad was constructed through Stony Clove, which people preferred to the bumpy stagecoach ride. Catskill Mountain House owner Charles Beach then built a cable funicular railroad 1630 ft up the Wall of Manitou to his grand hotel.

You begin a gradual ascent; wonderful ledges and cliffs adorn the steep side of the escarpment on the right, and the terrain drops to the valley on the left. Steadier climbing begins, but it is not far to the spur path leading left to Little Pine Orchard Picnic Area with a fireplace and a fine view of the Hudson River Valley. This is your destination. Retrace the route to your car.

If you have two cars, consider spotting a car at the Sleepy Hollow trailhead and hiking back down to the car from the North Lake beach picnic area. At the rear of the picnic area at the right end of a high wire-mesh fence, descend on a red-marked snowmobile trail for 0.6 mi to its junction with the horse trail (an old carriage road) that ultimately becomes the Sleepy Hollow Trail. Then continue left, heading north, with two switchbacks, for 2.6 mi to the Sleepy Hollow trailhead.

6. Palenville Overlook from Palenville and from South Lake

Round-trip distance: from Palenville, 7.7 mi (12.4 km);
    from South Lake, 5.0 mi (8.1 km)
Elevation change: from Palenville, 1300 ft (396 m);
    from South Lake, 500 ft (152 m)
High-point elevation: 2000 ft (610 m)
Difficulty: from Palenville, moderately strenuous; from South Lake, moderate
Maps: Page 30; Trail Conference Map 40 (P-4); USGS Kaaterskill 7.5'

Summary: From Palenville, this climb up the escarpment through interesting terrain leads to remnants of an old homestead at one of the spectacular lookouts in the Catskills. There are many intersecting trails, so you have the option of a loop or a traverse from the top to the bottom of the escarpment by spotting cars (see Hike 5).

South Lake offers a second delightful approach to Palenville Overlook from the top. This approach allows the hiker to visit the Catskill Mountain House site and Boulder Rock on the way, and cross the old Otis Railroad grade upon the return.

Access to area: From Palenville: at the intersection of NY 23A and NY 32A, travel west on NY 23A for 0.2 mi to Whites Road. Turn right, taking a left fork to the parking area. From the west, travel down NY 23A to Palenville. Travel about 0.7 mi to Whites Road, turn left and bear left at a fork to the parking area.

South Lake: From NY 23A in Palenville travel west to Haines Falls, turning right on County Route 18 at a large sign for North-South Lake state campground. Bear right after one block and travel 2.3 mi to the gatehouse. (There is a campground fee.) Bear right to South Lake, continuing past the beach parking area and bearing right to the last parking area. From the west, take NY 23A to Haines Falls and turn north (left) on County Route 18 at a large sign for North-South Lake state campground. See above directions.

Parking and trailhead: Palenville approach: Park in the new DEC parking area. Follow the yellow-marked spur trail about 0.2 mi, descending briefly, to the red-marked Harding Road Trail.

South Lake approach: Park across from the pavilion near the Catskill Mountain House sign and walk around the barrier.

Palenville Overlook from Palenville: Walk about 0.2 mi on a yellow-marked old woods road, descending left briefly on another road, then right up Harding Road Trail, once considered an engineering marvel because it switchbacked up the escarpment to the grand Kaaterskill Hotel on South Mountain.

As you ascend, views into Kaaterskill Clove begin to open up. The grade eases and you reach a trail register and a horse tie rail. The trail swings right at an excellent overlook with views of Kaaterskill Clove. Note the large fireplace built into the cliff.

This is beautiful territory through birch, hemlock, and pine woods, ascending gradually north by a Kaaterskill Creek tributary and crossing the dramatic (but often dry) rock-filled watercourse. The gradual ascent continues southwest to the escarpment edge, with high cliffs on your right. You ascend a switchback east-northeast and climb another 350 ft past interesting rock slabs to the junction with the Sleepy Hollow Horse Trail, 2.4 mi up Harding Road..

Turn right on the Sleepy Hollow Horse Trail, descending a short pitch and crossing a creek in shady hemlock woods. You lose elevation on gradual and moderate grades, then views across Kaaterskill Clove to High Peak and the Hudson appear when the trail swings southeast. Heading north again through mountain laurel, the trail is mostly level, then suddenly drops some 150 ft southeast to the Palenville Overlook junction.

Turn right on this yellow spur trail and hike a level 0.3 mi to the spectacular escarpment cliff. You arrive first at a clearing with a picnic table and fireplace. Continue along the path to the Palenville Overlook ledges. A large open area down the left path is certainly the spot for lunch, with its magnificent views and interesting stonework. Another ledge is to the right, with slightly different perspectives.

When you can tear yourself away, retrace your steps, turn left at the junction, return up to the Harding Road junction and continue left to descend the way you came. Be sure to note, near the bottom, that you turn left briefly, up a yellow-marked side road off Harding Road, then right to your car.

If you can, spot a car at the Sleepy Hollow trailhead (see Hike 5), making this a Harding Road–Sleepy Hollow loop. When returning on the spur trail from the overlook, turn right at the Palenville Overlook junction as you do in the hike below, taking the Sleepy Hollow Horse Trail back. It is only 0.2 mi longer than retracing via Harding Road. Turn right at the junction with Old Mountain House Road in 1.2 mi, following the Sleepy Hollow Horse Trail 2.6 mi back. (You need to spot a car, because the trailheads in Palenville are four miles apart.) Except for one area of ascent, the Sleepy Hollow Trail is level or gradual downhill to the Mountain Turnpike Road trailhead.

Palenville Overlook from South Lake: The trail heads east to the site of the Catskill Mountain House, with 180-degree views of the Hudson River Valley from the top of the cliffs. Climb the blue-marked Escarpment Trail to the right of the exhibit board. (A shorter red-marked trail bypasses Boulder Rock at the first junction.) Continue past Boulder Rock and Split Rock (Hike 2), proceeding west on the blue-marked Escarpment Trail. Enjoy the pleasant, level trek on South Mountain for 0.7 mi to another junction.

(Near the top of the mountain, to the right, you can see the foundation remains of the Kaaterskill Hotel, built by George Harding in 1880 after a tiff with Charles Beach, owner of the Catskill Mountain House. That lavish resort apparently had not provided a special diet for his daughter, so he built his own even more opulent hotel with rooms for 1000 guests, an orchestra, and Harding Road, painstakingly constructed to ascend the 1600-foot escarpment.)

Turn left for 0.6 mi at this junction, still following the blue-marked trail, and descend over 200 ft to a fourth junction. Turn left again, leaving the blue-marked Escarpment Trail. In another 200 ft, continue straight ahead at another junction, where the trail joins the one from Palenville.

Emerging from a hemlock woods, there are occasional views across Kaaterskill Clove to Kaaterskill High Peak. This section is a lovely trek surrounded by mountain laurel, with hiking on contour along mostly level terrain. Suddenly the trail descends steeply for 150 ft just before the junction to Palenville Overlook.

Turn right on the yellow-marked spur trail, a level 0.3 mi to the magnificent cliff tops beyond a clearing in the woods. One lookout is straight ahead past the clearing in the woods. A second one is at the end of the path heading left, which descends rock stairs to a stone wall and foundation.

This is a perfect spot for lunch with a view, sitting on one of three thrones created out of flat rocks—amazingly comfortable—on the edge of a cliff. Royalty never had it this good!

Retrace to the junction and turn right for 1.1 mi to a junction with the old Mountain House Road. Turn left for 0.5 mi and imagine bumpy stagecoaches bringing big-city escapees up these roads to the great cliff-top hotels.

If you spot a path left near the top, cross to the Otis Railroad Line, a more luxurious later approach to the Catskill Mountain House. Ascend to a clearing and follow a path, left, up to the Catskill Mountain House site. Turn right to return to the parking area.

If you continue up Mountain House Road, turn left at the chain-link fence, following the blue-marked Escarpment Trail to a clearing (the Otis Railroad bed is left). Walk across to a DEC sign, pass the barrier and ascend a scenic old road to a sign, "Historic Site—Catskill Mountain House." Turn right back to the parking area.

7. Kaaterskill Falls

Round-trip distance: 1.0 mi (1.6 km)
Elevation change: 350 ft (107 m)
Difficulty: Moderately easy; short hike with a steep beginning
Maps: Page 30; Trail Conference Map 40 (0-3); USGS Kaaterskill 7.5'

Summary: Kaaterskill Falls is one of New York's most spectacular waterfalls, plunging in two great sections from a famous escarpment named the Great Wall of Manitou into the Land of Falling Waters. Artists like Thomas Cole of the famous Hudson River School of landscape painting immortalized this area. In the nineteenth century, steamboats and railroads brought four presidents, industrialists, politicians, socialites, and seekers of beauty to this incomparable area where Rip Van Winkle slept away twenty years at Rips Boulder under the escarpment wall not far from Kaaterskill Falls.

▶ **Access to area:** From the east, travel up the scenic Kaaterskill Clove from Palenville on NY 23A, continuing 5.6 mi from its intersection with NY 32A. From the west on NY 23A past Haines Falls, travel 1.3 mi from North Lake Road.

Parking and trailhead: The large Molly Smith parking area is on the south side of NY 23A, uphill and 0.2 mi west of the Kaaterskill Falls trailhead. The trail begins at a near-horseshoe turn by a bridge on NY 23A, and is marked by a DEC sign on the north side of the road. **Caution:** The parking area is approximately 0.2 mi distant from the trailhead and the road offers little or no shoulder. Exercise great caution in crossing the road at the outset. Walk facing the traffic. You may want to walk in the gully when possible. ◀

As you begin your ascent past Bastion Falls and the cascades near the trailhead, take your time and enjoy the scenery, for this initial climb is steep and rocky.

Everything here is *big*—boulders, huge trees and their root systems, shale cliffs rising across the stream, and, of course, the falls. The water flows over red rock; dripping mosses sparkle in the sun. This is wild, rugged territory.

After what seems like a considerable hike, the trail opens to a breathtaking sight: a spectacular two-tiered waterfall dropping over massive overhanging ledges. The lower falls drops 85 ft and the very scenic upper falls 175 ft into a hidden intermediate pool. You're in a landscape of boulders and rocks of all shapes and sizes, some water-smoothed, some etched over the millennia with spray from the falls.

The trail ends in a viewing area at the base of a talus slope. Because of many deaths and injuries, the original Escarpment Trail to the intermediate-level pool and the top of the falls is closed.

Do not attempt to climb the falls. The beauty and popularity of this site sometimes divert visitors from the need for caution and restraint. Attempts to reach the natural amphitheater located at the intermediate-level pool, in particular, have resulted in fatal accidents. The talus rock found throughout the area is deceptively loose and slippery and thus exceedingly dangerous.

8. Catskill Mountain House and Lakeside Loop

Round-trip distance: 1.0 mi (1.6 km)
Elevation change: 50 ft (15 m)
Difficulty: Easy
Maps: Page 30; Trail Conference Map 40 (P-3); USGS Kaaterskill 7.5'

Summary: If you want a short, easy hike with spectacular views, visit the cliff top where a splendid hotel was constructed in 1824. This national historic site has exhibits describing its place in the heyday of Catskill Mountain great hotels.

▶ **Access to area:** On NY 23A from Palenville, travel up Kaaterskill Clove to Haines Falls. Turn north on County Route 18, turning right after one block, and continue for 2.3 mi to North-South Lake state campground. Past the gatehouse, turn right to South Lake, passing the beach parking area and bearing right at the fork to the end.

The North-South Lake state campground is closed from late October to early May. When the campground is closed, turn right after the gatehouse and drive to the parking area at the west end of South Lake. Walk 0.8 mi on the road, or hike the yellow-marked trail beginning beyond the guardrail. Follow the road to the last parking area, bearing right at a fork to a pavilion. Cross to the Catskill Mountain House sign.

If you are hiking the trail along South Lake, when you emerge at the beach, turn right to the road, then left to a fork where you bear right to the last parking area, just beyond.

Parking and trailhead: Park near the Catskill Mountain House sign. Walk east past the barrier. ◀

Much of the broad path to the Catskill Mountain House is on flat bedrock, passing old foundations and two stone posts. In 0.2 mi, you see ahead the open expanse of the meadow which was once a grove of great pine trees called Pine Orchard.

The Catskill Mountain House was built close to an enormous drop of 1600 ft to the Hudson River Valley. Imagine the old stationary engine Otis Railroad Line climbing this dramatic terrain, bringing presidents and the cream of society almost to the door of the great hotel. The railroad bed is to the left of this meadow, down a path. The train ride was a great improvement over the eight-mile bumpy stagecoach journey from Hudson River ships to North Lake. Night boats beamed great spotlights on the thirteen gleaming white Corinthian columns that adorned the front of the Catskill Mountain House.

The exhibit board describes the competing Kaaterskill Hotel and Laurel House, as well as nearby Kaaterskill Falls, one of New York's most dramatic waterfalls (see Hike 7).

Leaving the meadow, retrace back to the sign, "Historic Site: Catskill Mountain House," halfway along the path. Turn right here, following blue markers down a scenic old road past large mossy ledges. At the clearing past a barrier, turn left toward the lake. Follow a red-marked paved lane, a snow-mobile trail, left of the buildings into the woods. It stays close to the lake-side and leads to the shore at a lovely spot near several of the islands. The lane turns south and passes an amusing sight, a two-tiered giant ledge that looks like a whale's mouth, complete with many added pointed-rock "teeth" and a painted eye! The trail ends back at the parking area.

"I stand amid the eternal ways. "

—JOHN BURROUGHS

Northeast Catskills: Blackhead Range and Northern Escarpment

This area of the Catskills offers magnificent vistas east over the Hudson River Valley to Massachusetts, north to Albany, south to Slide and Table Mountains, west to the six Devils Path peaks. Climbs range from 1,000-foot ascents to escarpment overlooks to the 3,980-foot summit of Black Dome (1,780-foot ascent), the Catskill's third highest peak. The terrain here offers everything from long, level grades along the escarpment to vertical scrambles up the rugged ledges of the Blackhead Range. The many trails cut here since the completion of the Escarpment Trail in 1967 offer a variety of options for exploring all these areas surrounding Black Dome Valley, just a short trip south of Windham.

If you have time after a hike or want a change of pace, consider one of the attractions listed on page 32 or the following, which offers good swimming: **Batavia Kill Day-Use Area.** From NY 23 near Windham, drive south on NY 296 to Hensonville. Continue straight on County Route 40, then turn right for 2.0 mi to Maplecrest. At the junction of County Routes 40 and 56, turn left on County Route 56 for about 1.5 mi. Supervised swimming and picnic area.

9. Black Dome Mountain

Round-trip distance: 4.7 mi (7.6 km)
Elevation change: 1780 ft (543 m)
Summit elevation: 3980 ft (1214 m)
Difficulty: Strenuous
Maps: Page 51; Trail Conference Map 41 (O-2); USGS Freehold 7.5'

Summary: Black Dome Mountain, at 3980 ft, is the third highest mountain in the Catskills, after Slide at 4180 ft and Hunter at 4040 ft. The middle mountain in the three-peak Blackhead Range, Black Dome offers the hiker dramatic terrain to traverse, under ledges and by magnificent lookouts to the Hudson River Valley and Blackhead Mountain. From the summit, a spur trail south opens to outstanding views of the major Catskill mountain ranges. The characteristic profile of the Blackhead Range can be seen from Albany on clear days.

▶ **Access to area:** From NY 23 east of Windham, turn south on NY 296 to Hensonville. Where NY 296 swings right, continue straight on County Route 40, over a bridge, then right to Maplecrest. From NY 23A, turn north on Scribner Hollow Road, just east of Hunter ski area, to County Route 23C. Turn west, then north on County Route 40 to Maplecrest. In Maplecrest, continue east on County Route 56 (Big Hollow Road) to its end.

Parking and trailhead: Park in the large area to the right at the road's end. The trailhead is near the east end of the parking area, with red DEC trail markers leading southeast 150 ft to a trail register. ◀

The trail heads east along the bank of the pretty Batavia Kill, soon crossing a bridge. Look upstream to nearby remnants of an old mill. The trail crosses the brook on a new bridge at 0.4 mi and reaches the junction to Black Dome at 0.5 mi. Turn right on the red-marked trail.

The path ascends gradually and then increasingly steeply up to the col between Black Dome and Blackhead at 1.7 mi. Turn right at the col junction, continuing west on the red-marked Black Dome Range Trail (also known as the Blackhead Range Trail). Soon you reach a first overlook to Blackhead with expansive views over the northeastern Hudson River Valley. A scramble up rock ledges takes you to a second marvelous overlook south to Lakes Colgate and Capra, Kaaterskill High Peak, Roundtop Mountain, and North Mountain. Beyond lie the peaks of the Devils Path: Indian Head, Twin, Sugarloaf, and Plateau. Just ahead at another viewpoint, you can see Albany to the north on a clear day. The trail moderates briefly, then another scramble ends the major climbing. Gradual and then level grades continue across Black Dome's flat wooded summit. *Find the path, left,* to the open ledge with excellent views south to the Devils Path peaks and the Burroughs Range (Slide, Cornell, and Wittenberg) over Hunter Mountain. Near to the south are Onteora Mountain and Parker Mountain. This is a great spot for lunch. Retrace from Black Dome's summit, turning left at the junction in the col and left at the next junction.

If you're with a group and can spot a car at the end of Barnum Road in Maplecrest, continue west from Black Dome over Thomas Cole Mountain and down the ridge, which offers good views from Camels Hump and a lookout 1.0 mi from that trailhead. It is 3.7 mi from Black Dome's summit to Barnum Road. This makes a nice traverse with varied terrain. (See Hike 11.)

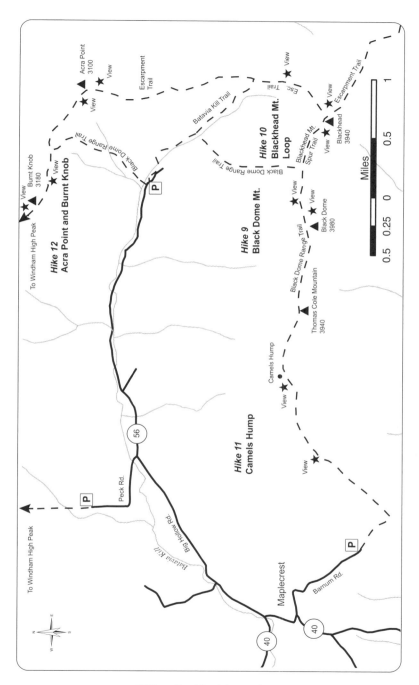

Hikes 9, 10, 11, and 12

10. Blackhead Mountain Loop

Round-trip distance: 4.5 mi (7.3 km)
Elevation change: 1740 ft (531 m)
Summit elevation: 3940 ft (1201 m)
Difficulty: Strenuous
Maps: Page 51; Trail Conference Map 41 (O-2); USGS Freehold 7.5'

Summary: Blackhead Mountain is the easternmost peak of the stately three-mountain Blackhead Range. Blackhead's summit tops out at 3940 ft, the same elevation as Thomas Cole Mountain to the west, creating a symmetry of peaks which on clear days can be appreciated from Albany. With Black Dome at 3980 ft, these are the third, fourth, and fifth highest mountains in the Catskills. This loop offers sweeping views in all directions, north and east from the Escarpment Trail, west and south from the open ledges on Blackhead's western slope.

▶ **Access to area:** From NY 23 east of Windham, turn south on NY 296 to Hensonville. Where NY 296 swings right, continue straight on County Route 40, over a bridge, then right to Maplecrest. From NY 23A, turn north on Scribner Hollow Road (just east of Hunter ski area) to County Route 23C. Turn west, then north on County Route 40 to Maplecrest. In Maplecrest, continue east on County Route 56 (Big Hollow Road) to its end.

Parking and trailhead: Park in the large area, right, at road's end. The trailhead is near the parking area at the east end, with red DEC trail markers leading southeast 150 ft to a trail register. ◀

Note: You can climb this loop either way. We chose the route described below, because it avoids the steep descent off Blackhead, which can be precarious. However, if you prefer less steep climbing, turn right on red-marked Black Dome Trail at the Batavia Kill junction 0.5 mi from the trailhead. Climb to the col between Blackhead and Black Dome, but turn left at the col junction on the yellow-marked Blackhead Mountain Spur Trail. After crossing Blackhead's summit, turn left on the blue-marked Escarpment Trail at the summit junction (visit the lookout ledge beyond the junction on the blue trail, then retrace your steps). Descend the steep section carefully, and turn left at the first junction (1.0 mi), and follow the yellow-marked Batavia Kill Trail back to trailhead.

The Blackhead Mountain Loop trail follows the bank of the Batavia Kill, heading east toward the Escarpment Trail. At a bridge crossing, note remnants of an old mill upstream. The trail crosses this brook again on a new bridge and reaches a junction at 0.5 mi. Continue straight on the yellow-marked Batavia Kill Trail, climbing gradually southeast to the Batavia Kill lean-to at 0.7 mi. From here, a steeper climb for 0.3 mi brings you to the blue-marked Escarpment Trail junction.

Turn right through a hemlock woods and begin a moderate ascent through a lovely birch forest. Great opportunities for breathers await you as you ascend. Sweeping views of the northern escarpment east to Arizona Mountain and the Hudson River Valley open up at Yellow Jacket Lookout half a mile from the junction. If you pick a very clear day, vistas as far as Albany are possible. The trail levels briefly near the marker indicating 3500-foot elevation. You climb the remaining 440 ft in less than half a mile to gain the summit of Blackhead.

Halfway there, a fine view to the north offers a welcome break. Take your time here and enjoy the wild terrain. Once we saw bear hunters way up here. The grade eases before the three-way junction; you will turn right on the yellow-marked Blackhead Mountain Spur Trail for the loop, but first turn left very briefly to a fine open area with good views. An inscription in the rock refers to this as "Steel Camp."

Retrace to the junction and hike across Blackhead's flat summit through thick evergreen and blueberries in season. Soon after you begin the descent, you come to a large open rock ledge with excellent views of Black Dome and beyond to Plateau, Hunter, West Kill, Rusk, and the Burroughs Range (Slide, Cornell, and Wittenberg). Here is a great spot for a well-needed break.

The trail descends steadily over ledges and then moderates to the col after passing the DEC marker indicating 3500-foot elevation. Turn right at this junction. After a steady descent for 0.4 mi to a spring to the right of the trail, the grade eases for another 0.3 mi and becomes gradual to the Batavia Kill Trail junction where you began the loop. Turn left here to return to your car.

11. Camels Hump

Round-trip distance: 4.0 mi (6.5 km); with extension, 5.0 mi (8.1 km)
Elevation change: 1400 ft (427 m)
High-point elevation: Camels Hump, 3525 ft (1075 m)
    (Thomas Cole Mountain summit, 3940 ft, or 1201 m)
Difficulty: Moderately strenuous
Maps: Page 51; Trail Conference Map 41 (N-2); USGS Hensonville 7.5'

Summary: Camels Hump is a prominent feature of Thomas Cole Mountain, a peak whose distinct profile is visible from Albany. Cole's long west-east ridge rises to the Caudal with a fine view of Devils Path peaks from a cliff top along the way. The terrain pitches upward to Camels Hump with views from two lookouts. These views are best when leaves are off the trees.

▶ **Access to area:** Just south of the junction of County Routes 40 and 56 in Maplecrest, turn east on Barnum Road (on a hairpin turn up a hill) for 0.9 mi to road's end. From the south, turn north in Tannersville on County Route 23C through East Jewett to County Route 40 (Maplecrest Road). Turn right. Turn right again on Hauser Road and right on Barnum Road to trailhead.

Parking and trailhead: Park in the area to the right, across from the DEC sign. The red-marked trail begins right, following an initial stony lane. (Avoid private property.) ◀

After crossing a small stream (note the dripping, mossy ledges, left) the trail levels on broad, flat rocks atop ledges. In 0.4 mi, turn left to the trail register at double markers, leaving the old road. Double markers mean a change in direction, and you'll soon note the trail ascending right at double markers again in rocky terrain, where the trail is obscure. Proceeding on large rocks through potentially muddy ground, another upgrade reaches state land.

Steeper climbing up the rocky mountainside brings you in one mile to a very steep final pitch upward under a dramatic rock overhang. At the top of this 50-foot rock outcrop, wonderful views greet you to Indian Head, Twin, Sugarloaf, Plateau and Hunter Mountains. Onteora Mountain is in the foreground. If you bushwhack right of the trail, in a few dozen yards there is a flat ledge to sit on and enjoy a better view. The terrain drops precipitously here!

A series of upgrades separated by short gradual sections finally levels at 1.3 mi at the Caudal, the "tailbone" of the camel, a welcome breather of level trail. After a short downgrade, the trail continues on gentle grades for 0.3 mi before gaining 200 ft to the hump, winding through ledges as you near the top at 2.0 mi.

A path right affords a view to the summit of Thomas Cole, now near to the east. This high mountain was named after Thomas Cole, founder of the Hudson River School of landscape painting. You can see Kaaterskill High Peak through trees to the southeast. A bit farther, a path left next to a boulder leads to another opening with good views to Burnt Knob, Windham High Peak, and the Windham ski area.

Back on the main trail, we recommend continuing down ledges to the extensive high meadow at 3450 ft, an interesting area to explore. When the climb to Thomas Cole begins again, above several initial ledges find a small path, right, at 2.5 mi to a flat rock with views to Plateau, Hunter, Rusk, and West Kill Mountains. Retrace your steps from here; summit views from Thomas Cole Mountain are almost completely obscured by trees and require 400 ft of additional ascent.

Views are terrific from Black Dome, however, so if you can spot a car at the end of Big Hollow Road at the Black Dome trailhead, you can continue, making this hike a traverse over two peaks. After climbing the 400 ft from the flat rock to Cole's summit in 0.4 mi, you lose 240 ft and ascend 280 ft up Black Dome in the 0.8 mi between the mountain summits. From there it is a 2.3-mile descent to the Black Dome trailhead. (See Hike 9 for descent to Black Dome's Big Hollow Road trailhead.)

12. Acra Point and Burnt Knob

Round-trip distance: Acra Point, 3.3 mi (5.3 km); Burnt Knob
  to north vista, 3.9 mi (6.3 km); hiking both, 5.2 mi (8.4 km)
Elevation change: 1000 ft (305 m) each; hiking both, 1300 ft (396 m)
Summit elevations: Acra Point, 3100 ft ((945 m);
  Burnt Knob, 3180 ft (970 m)
Difficulty: Moderate
Maps: Page 51; Trail Conference Map 41 (O-2); USGS Freehold 7.5'

Summary: Acra Point and Burnt Knob are lookouts from the Northern Section of the Escarpment Trail. The Northern Section was completed in 1967, later than other parts of the trail. Today, a race is held annually, beginning on NY 23 and ascending 1700 ft over Windham High Peak, across Burnt Knob and Acra Point, up 1100 ft to Blackhead's summit, down 1500 ft to Dutcher Notch, back up 1000 ft to Stoppel Point to North Lake, over 18 mi. Think about the race route as you hike these two "easier" sections of the Escarpment Trail.

Access to area: From NY 23 east of Windham, turn south on NY 296 to Hensonville. Where NY 296 swings right, continue straight on County Route 40, over a bridge, then right to Maplecrest. From NY 23A, turn north on Scribner Hollow Road (just east of Hunter ski area) to County Route 23C. Turn west, then north on County Route 40 to Maplecrest. In Maplecrest, continue east on County Route 56 (Big Hollow Road) to its end.

Parking and trailhead: The red-marked Black Dome Range Trail, providing access to the Acra Point/Burnt Knob area begins on the north side of Big Hollow Road, 0.1 mi west of the parking area.

A bridge over the Batavia Kill, 75 ft along the trail, leads to the trail register. The red-marked Black Dome Range Trail is to your right; note the marker on a tree. (Avoid an unmarked path straight ahead.) Rock-hopping over a tributary, the trail swings left along the tributary through lovely old hemlock. Ascending moderately through a birch woods, the footing is excellent. The trail recrosses the tributary. The grade eases and then levels near the escarpment junction at 1.0 mi.

Acra Point: Turn right to Acra Point on the blue-marked Escarpment Trail, and begin a steady ascent to your first lookout west off a short path on the right. More climbing to 0.3 mi rewards you with large ledges at the end of a path, right, offering fine views of Windham High Peak and Blackhead, Black Dome, and Thomas Cole Mountains.

Now you are treated to a level walk along the ridge top. A final upgrade takes you to Acra Point at 3100 ft, with an excellent open viewpoint to the northeast at 0.7 mi. Retrace your steps to the junction, turning left to your car.

Burnt Knob: From the junction, proceed west (left) on the blue-marked Escarpment Trail to Burnt Knob. You soon begin a steep climb of about 200 vertical feet, then swing south on moderating terrain to Burnt Knob's south lookout ledge, a few feet left on a spur path at 0.4 mi. The entire Blackhead Range is near to the south from this dramatic cliff top. Walk another 0.6 mi on contour at 3100 ft, and after a short, steep downgrade, look for a second 180-degree view north, just off-trail to the right. Windham High Peak is near to the west.

It is worth continuing west for another 0.4 mi. Circling below a rise in the escarpment and ascending briefly, you soon come to two very good open views to the Blackhead Range, Windham, and beyond to many mountains south and west. Here, you can retrace back to the junction, turning right on the red-marked trail back to your car.

Windham High Peak Loop Option: If you can spot a second car at the end of Peck Road off Big Hollow Road, 1.8 mi east of Maplecrest, continue west 1.3 mi to Windham High Peak from the last lookout above. The summit is a 600-foot ascent on varying grades, including two dips in the terrain en route. From the Windham summit, which has several excellent lookout ledges, it is a 3.1-mile descent to Peck Road, via the yellow-marked Elm Ridge Trail, left just beyond the path to the Elm Ridge lean-to. If you have spotted another car, this loop adds about two picturesque trail miles, compared to retracing your steps. (To walk back along Big Hollow Road to the parking area where you started would add another 3.5 mi.) See Hike 13 for details.

13. Windham High Peak

Round-trip distance: 6.6 mi (10.6 km)
Elevation change: 1784 ft (544 m)
Summit elevation: 3524 ft (1074 m)
Difficulty: Moderately strenuous
Maps: Page 57; Trail Conference Map 41 (M-2, N-2, N-1);
    USGS Hensonville 7.5'

Summary: A moderate ascent to a Catskill 3500-foot-plus peak. The trail features varied forests and terrain and offers excellent views, extending as far as Albany, from the summit ridge.
➤ **Access to area:** From NY 23, 2.0 mi east of the village of Windham.
Parking and trailhead: Turn north on Cross Road to access the large Forest Preserve parking lot on NY 23. The trailhead is across NY 23 at the DEC trail sign. ◀

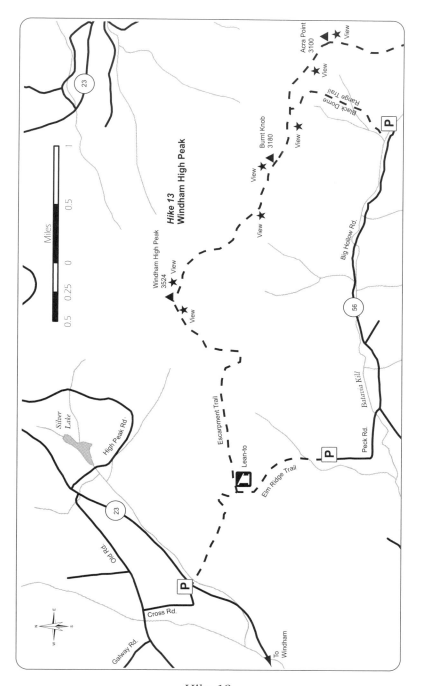

Hike 13
Windham High Peak

Windham High Peak
3524 ★ View

★ View

★ View

★ View

Burnt Knob
3180

★ View

★ View

Acra Point
3100

★ View

Black Dome
Range Trail

Escarpment Trail

Lean-to

Elm Ridge Trail

P

Silver
Lake

High Peak Rd.

23

Old Rd.

Cross Rd.

Galway Rd.

To
Windham

23

Peck Rd.

Batavia Kill

Big Hollow Rd.

56

P

P

Miles
0.5   0.25   0   0.5   1

N
W   E
S

Hike 13

The blue-marked Escarpment Trail crosses a bridge to a trail register. Heading south on the level, the trail swings left and climbs gradually, then more steeply, winding up to an old woods road. Turn right at this junction. Interesting ledges jut out of the hillside back in the woods. At a junction at 1.1 mi, continue on the blue-marked trail. Just beyond, the Elm Ridge lean-to is set on a picturesque rise, right, above rock ledges which invite exploration.

The trail climbs to a rise where camping was formerly permitted; views are only to the nearby area. Continue straight ahead, following blue trail markers and ascending gradual and moderate grades through many fine stands of large spruce trees. Each section gets more marvelously dark and dense. At 1.8 mi, half-log planks over a wet area lead to an entirely different area of open deciduous woods.

Ascending a short, steep pitch, the trail levels and stays on contour north and east below a ridge of the mountain. Crossing a tributary, you begin gradual and moderate climbing east on rocky terrain. Where the trail turns left, look for a view of Blackhead and Black Dome Mountains.

From here, the climb steepens up large ledges, but the grade moderates and nearly levels as you proceed north and east to the summit. Turning east at the summit, continue to a tiny spur path right for a lookout ledge facing the Blackhead Range. Continue east for another good overlook north and east, but the best is yet to come! Be sure to continue a bit farther, less than 0.1 mi and descending slightly, to a large open ledge with expansive views of the Hudson River Valley, an ideal spot for lunch. Albany's marble towers can be seen on clear days.

Windham is an excellent winter climb, with only three or four short, steep pitches. Most of the climb is on moderate and, near the top, even gradual grades. Views to the Blackhead Range are nearly constant in winter after emerging from the spruce forest.

If conditions are dry, the red-marked Elm Ridge Trail is a very attractive alternative approach to Windham

Blackhead Range from Acra Point
Henning Vahlenkamp

High Peak from nearby Maplecrest. From NY 23, take NY 296 south to Hensonville, continuing straight ahead on County Route 40 for 2 mi to Maplecrest. Turn left at the junction of County Routes 40 and 56 for 1.8 mi to Peck Road. Drive 0.8 mi to its end.

Much of the Elm Ridge Trail is on large, flat slabs of bedrock, making for great footing except when wet, when it is very slippery! Passing old stone walls, you ascend gradually to impressive rock outcrops and then cliffs at 0.8 mi. Turn right at the blue-marked Escarpment Trail, which ascends from NY 23. From here, refer to the description above to Windham High Peak.

Visit the Elm Ridge lean-to atop the cliff, an idyllic setting if you're not a sleep-walker!

14. Stoppel Point

Round-trip distance: 8.4 mi (13.5 km)
Elevation change: 2270 ft (692 m)
Summit elevation: 3420 ft (1043 m)
Difficulty: Strenuous
Maps: Page 60; Trail Conference Map 41 (P-2); USGS Freehold 7.5' and Kaaterskill 7.5'

Summary: This hike begins outside the Catskill Park Boundary and climbs the escarpment on what was an old road through the notch to the Jewett Valley. The northeast escarpment drops off to the side as you ascend. Outstanding views and an old plane wreck await you on the escarpment ridge.

▶ **Access to area:** On NY 32 (near the Catskill Game Farm), travel 0.2 mi north of Game Farm Road to Round Top/Purling sign at County Route 31 (Heart's Content Road). Turn left on Heart's Content Road for 4.0 mi (continue past the first intersection, crossing a bridge, to Maple Lawn Road beyond the fire station.) Turn left on Maple Lawn Road for 1.1 mi to Floyd Hawver Road. Turn left and immediately right on Stork Nest Road.

From NY 23, turn south in Acra on County Route 31 for about 4 mi. In Round Top, turn right on Maple Lawn Road for 1.1 mi to Floyd Hawver Road. Turn left and immediately right on Stork Nest Road.

Parking and trailhead: Travel 0.4 mi to a small parking area on the left side of Stork Nest Road just before it enters private property. The trail heads southwest past a large house. ◀

The yellow-marked trail follows an old route up to Dutcher Notch on a steadily ascending grade. It meanders next to and into a leaf-filled channel with hidden

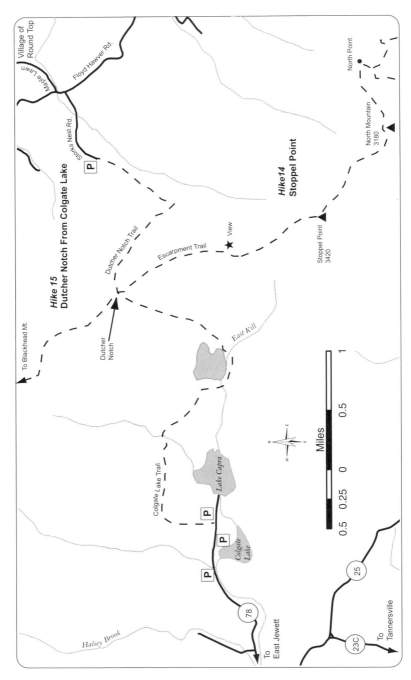

Hikes 14 and 15

rocks. In wet weather, the channel could be a drainage, so this hike is best reserved for dry periods.

The grade eases and the footing becomes very good as the trail swings northwest through hemlock woods at 1.3 mi. Dramatic moss-covered rock outcrops and views down the steep hillside through open woods make this section delightful. At 1.6 mi, a spring emerges from the rock. At 2.0 mi, you reach Dutcher Notch, a well-used spot for breaks.

Turning left on the blue-marked Escarpment Trail, you soon begin a steady ascent for about 0.3 mi, then the trail levels out for an equal distance with some loss of ascent. Steep ascents bring you to Milts Overlook, a spectacular view from an open ledge to the east and north over Roundtop Mountain and the Hudson River Valley.

From here, the trail is level through both deciduous and hemlock woods and then begins a moderate ascent to Stoppel Point. A plane wreck is left of the trail, its metal thoroughly gnawed by omnivorous porcupines. As the trail levels, you pass a fine overlook northwest to the Blackhead Range. The trail circles around the level Stoppel Point area to a good viewpoint east.

A DEC sign marks the summit at 3420 ft, 2.2 mi from Dutcher Notch. Here, retrace back to your starting point in Round Top village. (To continue to North Point is 1.7 mi and to North-South Lake state campground, 4.2 mi, if you spot a car at the campground.)

15. Dutcher Notch from Colgate Lake

Round-trip distance: Waterfall, 6.4 mi (10.3 km); Dutcher Notch, 8.6 mi (13.9 km)
Elevation change: 430 ft (131 m)
High-point elevation: 2530 ft (771 m)
Difficulty: Moderately easy; level but long
Maps: Page 60; Trail Conference Map 41 (O-3); USGS Kaaterskill 7.5'

Summary: A mostly-level woods ramble to a notch in the escarpment, by streams that converge at an old arching bridge, and by a meadow with a campsite and a lovely waterfall by an old rock foundation. The rugged notch terrain is scenic, but affords no view.

▶ **Access to area:** From NY 23A in Tannersville, turn north on County Route 23C to East Jewett. Turn east on County Route 78 in East Jewett and continue for 1.7 mi to the third DEC parking area (just before private road).

From NY 23, turn south on NY 296 to Hensonville. Leave NY 296, continuing straight on County Route 40. Turn right to Maplecrest. After crossing a bridge into Maplecrest, turn right, continuing on County Route 40 over a hill to County

Route 23C. Turn left to East Jewett. At a fire station, turn east on County Route 78 for 1.7 mi to the third DEC parking area on the left.

Parking and trailhead: Turn left into a large parking area. The trail begins at the rear of the grassy lot, crossing the meadow into woods to a trail register. ◀

Enjoy the view of the Blackhead Range as you cross the large meadow. The yellow-marked DEC Colgate Lake Trail winds through a mixed evergreen and deciduous woods, sometimes through wet or stony spots, but after passing a State Forest sign the footing becomes very good. In 2.5 mi, a short spur path leads to a large open swamp and you can see views of the escarpment ahead. Back on the main path, you pass through a thick grove of tiny hemlocks.

The trail turns left and crosses a bridge. Look for large crayfish in the deep pool. The trail parallels a river, soon reaching a fork in the waterway at an old arch bridge.

In a few minutes you reach a rocky stream flowing left with no obvious markers; rock-hop left and you'll soon see the trail (continuing in the same direction as the flow). There is an old rusty car way out here! Another small stream crossing on rocks leads to an open meadow. Be sure to go out into the meadow, for the wide-open area offers excellent mountain views. Blackhead Mountain, the fourth highest Catskill peak, is just north of here.

Continue east on the trail, formerly the East Jewett-Catskill road, near an old homestead with metal parts strewn about. Soon, look for an informal path forking right (you'll return to the trail which goes straight). A beautiful waterfall, swimming hole, and the stone foundation of an old mill are not far off-trail and worth seeing. Be careful of slippery rocks around the pool. (Retrace your steps here for a 6.4-mile round-trip.)

Continuing to Dutcher Notch, after a long level stretch northeast, you begin a very gradual upgrade. The trail becomes a lovely walk between rocky ledges and interesting landscape. Your destination at the Escarpment Trail junction is a clearing between Arizona Mountain 1.0 mi north and Stoppel Point 2.2 mi south. (See Hike 14.)

"How the contemplation of Nature as a whole

does take the conceit out of us!"

—JOHN BURROUGHS

Northeast Catskills: The Devils Path Peaks

The Devils Path is one of the most spectacular and challenging trails in the northeastern United States. Accessed off Platte Clove Road in the east, the path ascends five mountains and the shoulder of a sixth in 23.2 mi, descending near West Kill. Total ascent over the peaks is 7275 ft, and involves steeply descending and ascending the historic notches, cloves, and hollows that erosion created millennia ago.

The Devils Path begins off Old Overlook Road Trail, an old road used by Native Americans in the Revolutionary War for forced marches of prisoners to their stronghold at Echo Lake. Ascending Indian Head and Twin Mountains, the Path descends the cliffs of Sugarloaf to Mink Hollow, a route established before 1800 to transport hides from tanneries to the Hudson River port at Saugerties. It then plunges 1600 ft off Plateau Mountain to Stony Clove. The clove is so narrow that an artist wrote, ". . . in single file did we pass through it . . . this loneliest and most awful corner of the world." A walk up NY 214 from Devils Tombstone Campground beyond Notch Lake gives a sense of how narrow and wild the terrain was before a road was blasted through. The Devils Profile is high on a cliff of Hunter. The Devils Tombstone, a great boulder with a plaque commemorating the one hundredth anniversary of the establishment of the Forest Preserve, is on the east side of NY 214 at the primitive campground (which lacks electricity and plumbing).

A three-foot-wide narrow-gauge railroad was constructed through Stony Clove from Phoenicia to Hunter in 1882. The locals called it the "Huckleberry Line" because it moved so slowly that it was said a passenger could jump off, pick huckleberries, then climb back on. *The Great Train Robbery* was filmed here in 1903. If you have time after a hike or want a change of pace, consider one of the attractions listed on p. 32.

16. West Kill Mountain

Round-trip distance: 5.6 mi (9.0 km): through-trip, 7.7 mi (12.4 km)
Elevation change: 1700 ft (518 m)
Summit elevation: 3880 ft (1183 m)
Difficulty: Strenuous
Maps: Page 65; Trail Conference Map 41 (L-4); USGS Lexington 7.5'

Summary: A stiff climb to the sixth highest peak in the Catskills. You are rewarded with splendid views in all directions from two fine lookouts near the summit. Plan to spend time up here. If you can spot a car at the trailhead on Spruceton Road 3.8 mi east of NY 42, or at 6.9 mi at road's end, this hike is a terrific through-trip across the Devils Path of the West Kill Mountain section. (Or road-walk 3.0 mi.)

▶ **Access to area:** From NY 23A, take the side road south to Lexington. Turn south on NY 42 over the Schoharie Creek bridge and continue for 4.0 mi to West Kill hamlet. From NY 28 at Shandaken, turn north on NY 42 for 7.4 mi to West Kill hamlet. Turn east on Spruceton Road (County Route 6) for 6.9 mi.

Parking and trailhead: Park at road's end, 0.3 mi beyond the parking area on the north side of Spruceton Road and 0.1 mi beyond the parking area on the south side of the road. This is a snowplow turnaround, not a formal DEC parking area, but it accommodates several cars and its use is accepted as long as it's not winter. (If the area is full, park 0.1 mi back.) A trail register is beyond the barrier. ◀

Begin on the blue-marked Diamond Notch Trail, with a gradual grade that warms you up for the steady ascent of the Devils Path over the bridge at 0.7 mi. The pleasant stroll alongside the cascades of the West Kill brings you to Diamond Notch Waterfall. In summer, this is a welcome spot to stand under the spray of the falls at hike's end.

Cross the bridge and turn right on the red-marked Devils Path, following the south bank of the brook. The ledges, cascades, and pools tempt you to explore—be careful, because the ledges are slippery if wet. Soon, the trail swings left and begins the climb 1300 ft up to West Kill's east ridge.

The climbing becomes a steady and sometimes steep ascent. Most of your climb is in the next mile, so take your time and enjoy the attractive open woods with many large trees. The footing is good except for a rocky stretch climbing the remnants of an old road. The trail narrows as it slabs up the hillside to a small outcrop on the left, where cold and delicious water comes out of the rock from a wet-weather spring.

You'll have one level section before the trail swings south and begins several steep pitches up rock ledges. If you climb West Kill in winter, carry full crampons. The first ledge can be very icy, due to runoff in this north-facing area. You can bushwhack more safely a short distance east, which is especially important

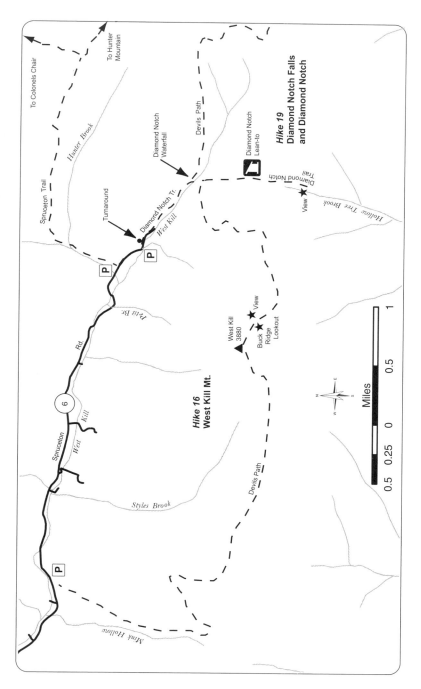

Hikes 16 and 19

on the descent.

The grade eases as you approach the ridgeline, and even levels in spots for welcome breathers. The "cave" overhang, topped with its own ecosystem of moss and trees, is reached just before the 3500-foot mark, a great spot for a break. Once you've climbed this rock outcrop at 1.4 mi, you will have completed most of the climbing and will be treated to a peaceful trek along the fern-filled east ridge for more than half a mile. The trail is a soft layer of crushed pinecones, like a walk on a nature trail.

It is especially gorgeous here on this high ridge on a sunny winter day. At about 3800 ft, copious snow blankets the landscape. You might catch a day when ice wraps each tiny branch, creating a shining canopy which clinks in the breezes.

A downgrade leads to the final short climb through lush mossy ledges to Buck Ridge Lookout. The views from this rock, which juts out over a drop, are unbeatable! To the north, the Blackhead Range and Windham High Peak decorate the skyline. Hunter Mountain ski area and fire tower dominate the east, and the Burroughs Range is prominent to the south, with Peekamoose and Table Mountains beyond. Diamond Notch Hollow is 2300 ft below you. Over Plateau Mountain, east, you can just see Overlook Mountain's two towers on a clear day. Bring binoculars.

A spur path on the other side of the trail leads to a boulder and wonderful views down to Spruceton Valley and across to Rusk and Evergreen Mountains. (The true summit, with no views, is 0.1 mi up to a wooded clearing with one of the Catskill's few markers identifying the actual summit, which is not obvious on many flat-topped peaks.) If you have not spotted a car, you will turn around here.

If you are doing the traverse to the end of the Devils Path, continue west along the level summit. Before a steady loss of 400 ft, in winter you have good views west through bare trees, standing on many feet of snow. A marker indicating the 3500-foot altitude is reached 0.7 mi from the summit, then the trail becomes a lovely, level walk through fern-filled woods for over half a mile. In 1.7 mi, rocky terrain rises ahead of you, an unexpected 200-foot ascent over a ridge spur, impressive terrain where water spurts out of a cleft in the ledges. Crossing the level field on top, look for a spur path, left, to limited views. You can see Mohonk's precipitous cliff to the south.

A sudden drop through steep ledges, a trek across a ferny level area, and a steady descent down the ridge takes you to a sign 3.0 mi from the summit. The trail switchbacks right and crosses some rivulets, descending briefly to Mink Hollow Brook. A grove of mature hemlock gives a sense of the early Catskills, before logging for the tannery industry began. The last mile is a lovely level trek through a young deciduous woods, with Mink Hollow dropping steeply to the left. (This is one of two Mink Hollows on the Devils Path.) The trail gradually ascends before the final downgrade brings you to the western trailhead of the spectacular Devils Path.

17. Hunter Mountain Loops from Spruceton Valley and from Stony Clove

Round-trip distance: from Spruceton Valley, 8.4 mi (13.5 km);
   from Stony Clove, 6.1 mi (9.8 km) trail, 1.6 mi (2.6 km) road
Elevation change: from Spruceton Valley, 1940 ft (592 m);
   from Stony Clove, 2040 ft (622 m)
Summit elevation: 4040 ft (1232 m)
Difficulty: from Spruceton Valley, moderately strenuous;
   from Stony Clove, strenuous
Maps: Page 70; Spruceton Valley to Hunter summit: Trail Conference Map 41
   (L-4); USGS Lexington 7.5' and Hunter 7.5'. Stony Clove to
   Hunter summit: Trail Conference Map 41 (M-4); USGS Hunter 7.5'

Summary: From Spruceton Valley, the hike combines four trails over Hunter Mountain, the Catskill's second highest peak. This hike is easier than many other "strenuous" hikes because there are no challenging steep ledges to negotiate and the ascent is spread out over 4.6 mi. The route allows you to enjoy brooks, a lovely waterfall, fine overlooks, two lean-tos, and a fire tower.

From Stony Clove: If the hiker prefers steep scrambles, this route includes the Devils Path, which offers a 50-foot area of cliffs, ledges, and overhangs called the Devils Portal. Higher up, the trail mellows into a long, level trek, then a gradual ascent through beautiful forest to the summit.

Access to area: Spruceton Valley: From NY 23A, turn south on NY 42 and continue for 4 mi to West Kill hamlet. From NY 28 in Shandaken, turn north on NY 42 for 7.4 mi to West Kill. Turn east on Spruceton Road (County Route 6) for 6.7 mi.

From Stony Clove: From NY 23A just east of Hunter village, turn south on NY 214 for 1.3 mi to Becker Hollow trailhead. From NY 28 in Phoenicia, turn north on NY 214 for 12.2 mi.

Parking and trailhead: From Spruceton Valley: Park in either of the DEC parking areas, located at 6.7 mi and 6.9 mi. Walk along the road to its end at 7.0 mi. The trail register is beyond the barrier.

From Stony Clove: We suggest parking at Becker Hollow to avoid the day-use parking fee at Notch Lake. Spot a second car there to avoid walking along the roadside (although the trek by beaver ponds, rocky mountainsides, and Notch Lake is very pleasant).

Hunter Mountain Loop from Spruceton Valley. Your first trail is the blue-marked Diamond Notch Trail, a fine warm-up for the steady climbing which awaits you on the Devils Path. For the first 0.7 mi, you walk along the north bank of West Kill brook on gradual grades. At the clearing you are treated to beautiful

Diamond Notch waterfall. You can scramble down to the waterfall and wade under the cooling spray on a hot day. (Ledges across the stream are slippery if wet).

Sign the trail register and follow red-marked Devils Path left of the register over a rise (do not cross the bridge). A small brook is crossed on rocks. (This is tricky in winter; bushwhack upstream for the best crossing.) Several more streams can make this part of the trail wet. A steady upgrade takes you to Geiger Point at 1.5 mi on a spur trail, right, a great overlook ledge facing Southwest Hunter Mountain over West Kill Valley, a fine spot to break.

The trail now swings south on level and descending terrain between Hunter and Southwest Hunter. A short climb takes you to a level section. (You may spot a cairn, which marks the old narrow-gauge railroad bed. This slabs up Southwest Hunter Mountain and is a good approach for ascending this trailless mountain.) Descend to a clearing and brook; you may see remnants of railroad equipment, which brought lumber down to a Diamond Notch sawmill. A spring outflow and the Devils Acre lean-to soon greet you. The Devils Path continues 300 ft to the yellow-marked Hunter Mountain Spur Trail on the left. Follow this on gradual grades through attractive conifer forest. (The Devils Path continues down Hunter Mountain to the Devils Tombstone Campground. See the second loop option, p. 69.)

In 0.3 mi, the trail begins its swing to the west. Balsam woods increasingly close in around you. In winter, this high area is beautiful, with snow sometimes completely blanketing the evergreens. You gain an easy 500 ft of ascent from the lean-to, before a long level section reaches the Becker Hollow Trail junction at 1.4 mi. Be sure to follow the side path on the left to two excellent lookouts atop a cliff.

Back at the junction, turn left on the blue-marked trail 0.3 mi to the summit. Enjoy the 360-degree views in the heart of the Catskill high peaks from the top of the fire tower. The ski area is way below you to the north; West Kill to the west; Plateau, Sugarloaf, Twin, and Indian Head Mountains on the Devils Path are nearby to the southeast. Thomas Cole, Black Dome, and Blackhead are northeast, Kaaterskill High Peak and Roundtop are east. The Burroughs Range is south.

Turn right to descend 400 ft via the blue-marked Spruceton Trail, on moderate and nearly level grades, to the Colonels Chair junction. (The Colonels Chair Trail loses about 500 ft of ascent in 1.1 mi. See Hike 18.) Continuing on the blue-marked trail, you soon reach the John Robb lean-to and a good view west from a boulder. In another 0.1 mi, a 300-foot spur trail ends at a good spring, if you're running low on water.

The descent steepens from here, curving down the mountain on rocky trail to a clearing halfway down. Continue on the blue-marked trail, left, which soon swings west, descending moderately to a tributary of Hunter Brook, crossing on a wide bridge and passing a trail register. For another 0.3 mi you walk near the scenic brook to the trailhead. Turn left on the road for 0.2 mi back to your car.

This is an especially nice winter hike, because there are no very steep ledges along this loop. The high evergreen forest along the Hunter Mountain Spur Trail is very beautiful in winter.

Hunter Mountain Loop from Stony Clove: Walk 1.6 mi south on NY 214 past Notch Lake. Go through the picnic area and beyond the dam to cross a bridge to the trailhead. The trail register is up the trail.

You soon enter wild and very scenic territory as you walk below mossy rock walls. The red-marked Devils Path earns its name here, as you begin scrambling up the 50-foot vertical zone known as the Devils Portal. Note carefully a left turn atop a ledge, staying on the red-marked trail. (An old path diverges to the right.)

From here, the path climbs on varying grades to 3500 ft, where suddenly the ascent ends as you circle around a large ledge. You begin a long, level trek through a beautiful birch woods, staying on contour along the sloping mountainside. At 2.2 mi, you reach the Hunter Mountain Spur Trail.

Turn left first and visit the Devils Acre lean-to and spring. Back at the junction, follow the yellow-marked trail, which is a delightful gradual ascent through a dense hemlock and balsam forest. It hardly seems as if you've ascended another 500 ft, when you arrive at the Becker Hollow junction at the site of the old fire tower. Here, be sure to turn left briefly for a spectacular lookout ledge, a great place to eat lunch.

Return to the Becker Hollow junction. Do not descend here via Becker Hollow, but turn left toward the summit on the blue-marked trail for 0.3 mi. Enjoy the 360-degree views from the fire tower. All the mountains you see are identified in the loop approach from Spruceton Valley described earler.

Your descent route begins near the fire tower, on the side opposite the cabin. The yellow-marked scenic spur trail to Becker Hollow descends into the woods and then heads southeast for 0.3 mi to the Becker Hollow Trail.

Turn left on the blue-marked trail, where you'll want to take your time descending on loose rock. The trail does improve markedly as the grade moderates, and the trek becomes very scenic through a beautiful forest.

Crossing a brook, you come upon an old 50-foot concrete dam. This area is a fine spot to take a needed break after descending 2,000 ft! Explore the dam and enjoy the cascading brook. A big footbridge is 0.3 mi from the trailhead. The level path is very attractive above the brook and through old meadows. Sign out at the trail register by the large stone arch, an unexpected landmark at a trailhead!

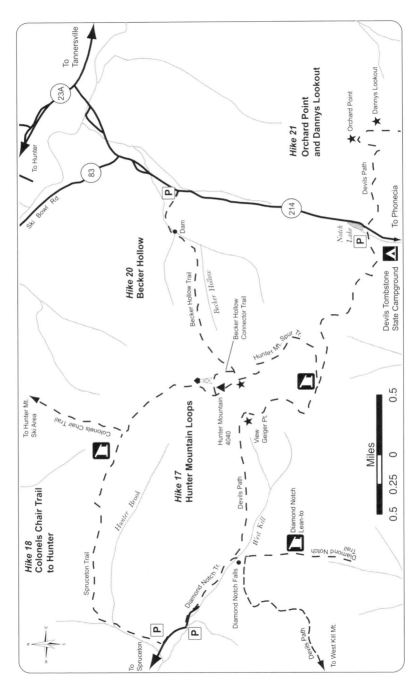

To Tannersville

To Hunter

23A

83

Ski Bowl Rd.

P

Hike 20
Becker Hollow

Dam

Becker Hollow Trail

Becker Hollow

Becker Hollow
Connector Trail

214

Hike 21
**Orchard Point
and Dannys Lookout**

Orchard Point

Dannys Lookout

★

Devils Path

*Notch
Lake*

P

To Phonecia

Devils Tombstone
State Campground

Hunter Mt. Spur Tr.

To Hunter Mt.
Ski Area

Colonels Chair Trail

Hike 18
**Colonels Chair Trail
to Hunter**

Hunter Mountain
4040

★

View
Geiger Pt.

★

Hike 17
Hunter Mountain Loops

Hunter Brook

Spruceton Trail

Devils Path

West Kill

Diamond Notch
Lean-to

Diamond Notch
Trail

Diamond Notch Tr.

Diamond Notch Falls

P

P

To Spruceton

Devils Path

To West Kill Mt.

N
E
S
W

Miles

0.5   0.25   0   0.5

Hikes 17, 18, 20, and 21

18. Colonels Chair Trail to Hunter Summit

Round-trip distance: 4.2 mi (6.8 km)
Elevation change: 940 ft (287 m)
Summit elevation: 4040 ft (1232 m)
Difficulty: Moderate
Maps: Page 70; Trail Conference Map 41 (M-3); USGS Hunter 7.5'

Summary: On Saturdays and Sundays from early July to Columbus Day, and in winter, you can ride the Sky Ride ski lift to Summit Lodge, then hike the DEC-marked Colonels Chair Trail. This trail leads to the 4040-foot summit and fire tower of Hunter Mountain. Snowshoes are available for rent at the Main Lodge.

▶ **Access to trail:** Locate the Skyride ski lift at Hunter Mountain Main Lodge, off NY 23A in the village of Hunter.

Parking and trailhead: Follow signs to Sky Ride. Verify time of the lift's last descent and allow plenty of time. The Skyride itself takes eleven minutes to ascend; the same is true for the descent. Normal hours of operation are 10:00 A.M.– 5:00 P.M. ◀

Once you've ascended on Sky Ride, follow signs for the Z lift. Keep going straight, past the Z lift (on the right). Follow Hunter Mountain yellow markers to a sign that guides you left to the Colonels Chair Trail. Sign the trail register. The yellow-marked DEC trail forks left and ascends. Varying grades bring you to a junction with the blue-marked Spruceton Trail, where you turn left. It is now 1.0 mi to the summit fire tower.

Level trail gives you a breather, then short upgrades through attractive woods lead to the large clearing with an old cabin and renovated fire tower. Panoramic 360-degree views north to the Blackhead Range, east to Kaaterskill High Peak, west to West Kill Mountain, south to the Burroughs Range, and southeast to other Devils Path peaks await you.

For excellent views south from an open rock ledge, leave the southeast edge of the fire tower clearing (across from where you entered) and walk 0.3 mi through level evergreen woods. Turn right at the Becker Hollow Trail junction and follow an informal path to two lookout ledges.

When you retrace your steps back to the fire tower, remember that the Colonels Chair junction is only 1.0 mi from the tower, then a right turn. Stay alert for it. We met a man who had descended all the way to Spruceton Road, looking for the village of Hunter 18 miles away! We talked to a woman in Spruceton who said, "You wouldn't believe how many people end up here. I charged one to drive him back."

The Summit Lodge area offers a self-guided nature tour, a 1.0-mile loop trail on level ground. Follow the white arrows and look for brown and white station numbers that feature the history, geology, flora, and fauna of this region.

19. Diamond Notch Falls and Diamond Notch

Round-trip distance: Waterfall, 1.4 mi (2.3 km); notch, 2.8 mi (4.5 km)
Elevation change: Waterfall, 200 ft (61 m); notch, 550 ft (168 m)
High-point elevation: Waterfall, 2300 ft (701 m); notch, 2650 ft (808 m)
Difficulty: Moderate; easy to falls
Maps: Page 65; Trail Conference Map 41 (L-4); USGS Lexington 7.5'

Summary: An easy hike along a beautiful mountain brook to a 12-foot waterfall and cascades. The perfect destination for a hot summer day. A harder ascent, beyond, to a rugged notch between West Kill and Southwest Hunter Mountains, with a talus slope and rock ledges in the narrow col. A lean-to is set in a picturesque setting below the notch.

▶ **Access to area:** From NY 23A, take the short side road south into Lexington. Turn south on NY 42 and travel 4 mi to West Kill hamlet. Turn east on Spruceton Road (County Route 6) for 6.9 mi.

Parking and trailhead: Park at the road's end, 0.3 mi beyond the DEC parking area on the north side of Spruceton Road and 0.1 mi beyond the DEC parking area on the south side of the road. This is a snowplow turnaround, not a formal DEC parking area, but it accommodates several cars and its use is accepted as long as it's not winter. A trail register is beyond the barrier gate. ◀

The Diamond Notch Trail follows the cascading waters of the West Kill for 0.7 mi. It is almost impossible to pass by some areas without going down and wading in the pools. This is the old woods road connecting Stony Clove to West Kill and Spruceton through rugged Diamond Notch. You gradually ascend toward a clearing, where the 12-foot Diamond Notch waterfall plunges to a shallow pool near a bridge. Save this hike for a very hot day. Standing under the chilly spray is a terrific way to cool off. There are lots of areas to explore from the Devils Path, right, across the bridge. Be careful of slippery ledges.

If you decide to continue 0.7 mi up to Diamond Notch's view, be advised that the footing is rocky. You will climb 350 ft to the Diamond Notch lean-to from the waterfall in 0.5 mi. The lean-to is off trail on a spur path to the left.

After enjoying this scenic setting, continue through the narrowing notch, which crosses an interesting tumble of talus rocks, amazingly stable on the steep west face of Southwest Hunter Mountain. Views begin to open up to the east ahead of you. The terrain is dramatic, with a sharp drop right and ledges adorning West Kill Mountain just across. Continue to a large, flat rock, almost 0.1 mi from the height of land at 2650 ft. The route is fully open for good views. Retrace from here. (The trail ahead descends steadily down Diamond Notch Hollow on rocky ground for 1.3 mi to the trailhead off NY 214 in Lanesville.)

20. Becker Hollow

Round-trip distance: 1.1 mi (1.8 km)
Elevation change: Negligible
Difficulty: Easy
Maps: Page 70; Trail Conference Map 41 (M-4); USGS Hunter 7.5'

Summary: A lovely stroll through woods above a brook to an old 50-foot concrete dam.

▶ **Access to area:** From NY 23A (east of Hunter village), turn south on NY 214 for 1.3 mi.

   Parking and trailhead: Park on the west side of the road at the large DEC parking area. The trail register is at the stone arch. ◀

The blue-marked DEC trail passes under an interesting large stone arch, perhaps the remaining landmark of an old estate. Owing to damage, the top of the arch has been removed. The large meadow-like area beyond looks as if it had been cleared at one time for a homestead or farm.

The nearly level trail passes high above a brook and, at 0.3 mi, crosses the brook on a footbridge. Beyond, the trail curves left and passes a three-tiered cascade. At 0.4 mi, the trail arrives at a 50 ft concrete dam on which one can walk.

Retrace from here or follow the trail into the attractive forest a bit farther. (The trail soon begins a relentless ascent for 2000 ft to the summit of Hunter Mountain.)

Before crossing the bridge on your return, look for the path straight ahead, which takes you to an idyllic spot overlooking the pretty brook. Retrace and turn left over the bridge to return.

Becker Hollow Trail

21. Orchard Point and Dannys Lookout

Round-trip distance: Orchard Point, 2.5 mi (4.0 km);
   Dannys Lookout, 2.8 mi (4.5 km)
Elevation change: 1600 ft (488 m)
High-point elevation: 3600 ft (1098 m)
   (true summit of Plateau Mountain, 3840 ft or 1171 m)
Difficulty: Strenuous; a short, very steep ascent
Maps: Page 70; Trail Conference Map 41 (M-4); USGS Hunter 7.5'

Summary: Splendid views of Hunter Mountain and vistas from south to north from two overlooks. Choose a very clear day to see for many miles across myriad mountain ranges and valleys. An ascent to Orchard Point on Plateau Mountain, 1600 ft in only 1.3 mi, means steady and sometimes steep climbing.

▶ **Access to area:** From NY 23A, turn south on NY 214 east of the village of Hunter. Continue for 2.9 mi, just past Notch Lake. From NY 28, turn north on NY 214 in Phoenicia for 10.6 mi.

Parking and trailhead: Park north of the Devils Tombstone Campground at the parking area on the west side of NY 214, next to Notch Lake. Pay fee at the Campground office, 0.2 mi south of the parking area. Cross NY 214 to the trailhead, ascending log steps to the trail register. ◀

Red DEC trail markers guide you up the Devils Path, which quickly fulfills its name, becoming a very steep ascent. Take your time as you switchback this steepest section, both on the ascent and the descent. The trail then slabs across the mountainside on moderating grades, with the terrain dropping ever more steeply to the right. This steepness has caused rock slides halfway up, which are interesting features to walk across on this trail. The ascent briefly becomes gradual here.

After turning left at about 1.0 mi (note trail markers), you ascend steeply and then swing left again; the trail moderates and levels through a flat wet area. Watch carefully for markers here. The trail swings right through a ledge and ascends moderately on rocky trail for the last 0.2 mi.

As you arrive below Orchard Point at 1.3 mi, one final challenge remains. The climb onto the large, open ledge is a stretch! If necessary, you can find a path below the ledge to its right, which leads to a slightly more manageable scramble. Above, find a path straight through the evergreen and circle back to Orchard Point, to avoid walking next to the drop.

Enjoy the well-earned, magnificent vistas in the cool breezes on this broad, open rock ledge. Be sure to continue across the ferny summit plateau 0.1 mi to Dannys Lookout, with excellent views north to Blackhead, Black Dome, and Thomas Cole Mountains and the escarpment. Retrace from here. Descend with care; the grade steepens toward the end on pebble-strewn trail.

(From Dannys Lookout, the trail continues for another two miles across the flat, wooded summit of Plateau to the technical summit at 3840 ft, off-trail in the woods. From that side of the mountain, a good view east is reached 0.2 mi down toward Mink Hollow. That viewpoint is 0.9 mi and 1240 ft up the Devils Path from Mink Hollow.)

22. Sugarloaf Mountain Loop

Round-trip distance: 7.0 mi (11.3 km)
Elevation change: 1850 ft (564 m)
Summit elevation: 3800 ft (1159 m)
Difficulty: Difficult
Maps: Page 79; Trail Conference Map 41 (N-4); USGS Hunter 7.5'

Summary: This loop over Sugarloaf Mountain is one of the most dramatic trails in the Catskills and in the Northeast. Intricate stonework in quarries, great views, cliffs, rock ledges and outcrops of the Devils Path make this hike a truly spectacular experience. In winter, the steep areas can be hazardous. Always carry full crampons. It is important to choose a day when snow texture packs well, allowing you to make "steps" upward with snowshoes. Devils Path peaks especially should be avoided after a thaw and refreeze, when snow becomes hard and glazed, or if snow is too soft for stable footing. Early and late in the winter season, the steep ledges can be icy without a protective layer of snow.

▷ **Access to area:** From NY 23A in Tannersville, turn south on Depot Road (at light) to County Route 16. From Hunter, travel east on NY 23A to Bloomer Road (County Route 16), turning right. At the sign to Elka Park, continue on Elka Park Road south, forking left at Green Hill Road. Continue past Park and Mink Hollow Roads and cross the bridge spanning the Roaring Kill (take a moment to look at this magnificent mountain stream). Road walk briefly if bridge is out.

The trailhead also can be approached from West Saugerties via a steep ascent up Platte Clove Mountain Road. This road is closed in winter.

Parking and trailhead: Park in the DEC parking area, right, beyond the Roaring Kill bridge. The trail begins at the parking area. ◁

The trail ascends gradually through an open forest, reaching a junction at 0.3 mi. Turn right on the blue-marked trail, a pleasant walk nearly on the level through open woods. After crossing two drainages, you enter a hemlock woods still on very gradual grades. At a hairpin turn at 0.8 mi, mossy 20-foot cliffs loom over large man-made rock structures and walls. They are extensive, so explore a bit to the west also.

Now the trail climbs steeply at times through large hemlocks and then switchbacks toward a cave in the mountainside, turning right below the rock outcrops, then climbing them. At about 2750 ft, the trail heads toward Mink Hollow for 0.5 mi on nearly level grades, offering views west and north through the trees to Plateau and Spruce Top Mountains. At a good open view to Plateau, the trail descends as it switchbacks east, then heads through a cleft in the rock and turns west toward the col between Sugarloaf and Plateau. A good bridge crosses a tributary. In 2.9 mi, you've reached the Devils Path, where you turn left on the red-marked trail. (Trail, right, soon reaches the Mink Hollow lean-to to the left.)

Now a really stiff ascent begins—1200 ft in 1.0 mi to the summit. You ascend alongside tank-sized sedimentary boulders tipped crazily on the steep mountainside. The trail goes underneath rock slabs then traverses a short, narrow ledge. Soon you arrive at a smooth natural wall extending north and south. This is spectacular territory! The trail turns north (left), under the towering overhang, and soon ascends on ledges to the top.

Caution! It is easy to miss the route the trail ascends most safely. The trail appears to continue below the cliff to an ascent farther on. If you reach a rock over a crevice, then a large, very precarious, vertical ledge, retrace your steps to locate the safer ascent. Look for red markers, one on a large tree below and another on a small tree at the cliff top.

The trail turns right along the cliff top. Proceed with caution. Soon, it goes through a "lemon squeezer" (a narrow passage through rocks) and a variety of scenic scrambles. Passing the 3500-foot mark, the ascent moderates through meadow-like areas that can be wet. The trail arrives at a big boulder, which offers a fine lookout west to Plateau Mountain.

Watch for a yellow-marked spur trail, right, 0.1 mi up the trail from here, which takes you to the main summit viewpoint. On a sizable rock ledge, enjoy expansive vistas to the south and east. Retrace to the red-marked Devils Path and turn right through fragrant hemlock-balsam woods across the summit. (A second spur path leads to a wooded clearing with no view.)

The descent begins gradually until you reach the first of several steep drops through rock ledges—an all-body workout! You walk through a narrow L-shaped section of rock to discover weather-rounded edges of sedimentary walls separating like drifting continents. Two excellent views east to Twin Mountain show similar rocky terrain, where the Devils Path ascends 860 ft—a challenge for another day.

At the junction in the col, turn left and descend on the blue-marked trail for 0.4 mi to a sign, where the trail turns left into a meadow and wetlands, with good views back to Twin and Sugarloaf Mountains. As you enter a forest of mature hemlock and beech, note bear clawings on the large beech trees (bears like beechnuts). Soon the trail reaches a steep bank and runs alongside a cascading brook, crossing it on a fine new bridge.

If you think you've seen wonders up to now, wait until you reach a massive quarry and stonework complex with expansive views north and east. (See Hike 23.) In 0.7 mi you're back at the junction where you started the loop. Turn right on the yellow-marked trail back to your car.

Sugarloaf also can also be approached from NY 212 in Lake Hill, a few miles west of Woodstock. Drive 2.9 mi north on Mink Hollow Road. The trail follows the old route for transporting hides from the port at Saugerties to Catskill tanneries. Given the rocky footing, it's hard to imagine this trail as a transportation route. Much of it, though, is pleasant walking on moderate or gradual grades for 2.5 mi to Mink Hollow lean-to and the Devils Path. This route gains 1090 ft to the col at 2600 ft.

23. Magical Quarry on Sugarloaf

Round-trip distance: 2.0 mi (3.2 km)
Elevation change: 200 ft (61 m)
High-point elevation: 2200 ft (671 m)
Difficulty: Moderately easy
Maps: Page 79; Trail Conference Map 41 (N-4); USGS Hunter 7.5'

Summary: This is a fascinating and unexpected place, not far up a mountain trail, featuring extensive stonework crafted out of the remnants of an old quarry. The quarry overlooks Kaaterskill High Peak and the Plattekill Clove. Not to be missed!

▶ **Access to area:** From NY 23A in Tannersville, take Depot Road south (at light) to County Route 16. From Hunter, travel east on NY 23A to Bloomer Road (County Route 16) and turn right. At the sign to Elka Park, continue on Elka Park Road, south, forking left at Green Hill Road. Continue past Park and Mink Hollow Roads and cross the bridge spanning the Roaring Kill (take a moment to enjoy this magnificent mountain stream). Road walk briefly if bridge is out.

The trailhead also can be approached from West Saugerties via a steep ascent up Platte Clove Mountain Road. This road is closed in winter.

Parking and trailhead: Park in the DEC parking area, right, beyond the Roaring Kill bridge. The trail begins from the parking area. ◀

This recently created trail heads to a remarkable place in its first mile. Once the site of industry, a very extensive quarry, it is now the scene of creative activity by playful and skillful persons unknown. Leaving the parking area on a yellow-marked trail, you ascend gradually through open woods to a junction at 0.3 mi.

Turn left here on the blue-marked trail. There is a short, initial climb and then the grade eases, passing a large boulder. Another short, steep pitch up Mudd Quarry brings you to a more level section through a hardwood forest to a shady hemlock grove. Look carefully for trail markers, left, to guide in your descent.

At 1.0 mi, you emerge suddenly onto Dibbles Quarry, with expansive views to Kaaterskill High Peak, Roundtop Mountain to its west, Schoharie Valley below, and the Hudson River Valley in the background. You can take a seat to rest from the hike, view the northern Catskills and contemplate who built this magical stonework complex. Across from the amazingly comfortable seats are a stone fireplace with overhanging stone wood box and slab benches. A child's rock seat is left of the triangular throne. Other fire pits are behind this area. A short scramble down to the right takes you to an enormous rock overhang with its own fire pit.

(If you wish to explore the trail farther, it crosses a new bridge in 0.2 mi over a Schoharie Creek tributary and climbs above it through pretty woods. If you look carefully, you may see bear marks on beech trees. The trail winds into an open meadow 0.6 mi from the quarry, with views of Sugarloaf and Twin Mountains.)

After exploring the quarry to your heart's content, retrace your trail, turning right at the junction and back to the trailhead.

24. Twin Mountain from Pecoy Notch and from Jimmy Dolan Notch

Round-trip distance: via Pecoy Notch to the true summit, 5.3 mi (8.5 km); via Jimmy Dolan Notch to the southeast summit, 4.6 mi (7.4 km)
Elevation change: via Pecoy Notch, 1690 ft (515 m); via Jimmy Dolan Notch, 1580 ft (482 m)
Summit elevation: 3640 ft (1110 m)
Difficulty: Difficult with challenging steep areas
Maps: Page 79. Via Pecoy Notch: Trail Conference Map 41 (N-4), USGS Hunter 7.5'. Via Jimmy Dolan Notch: Trail Conference Map 41 (O-4); USGS Kaaterskill 7.5', Woodstock 7.5', and Bearsville 7.5'

Summary: We can't decide which of the two wonderful approaches to Twin Mountain is better, so we offer both, each ascending the Devils Path with everything that magnificent trail offers: steep ledges, rock overhangs, beautiful views. The approach from Pecoy Notch is challenging, and is recommended for experienced hikers. It has some of the steepest parts of the entire 23.2-mile Devils Path. The approach from Jimmy Dolan Notch is just normally steep.

▶ **Access to area:** From NY 23A in Tannersville, turn south on Depot Road (at

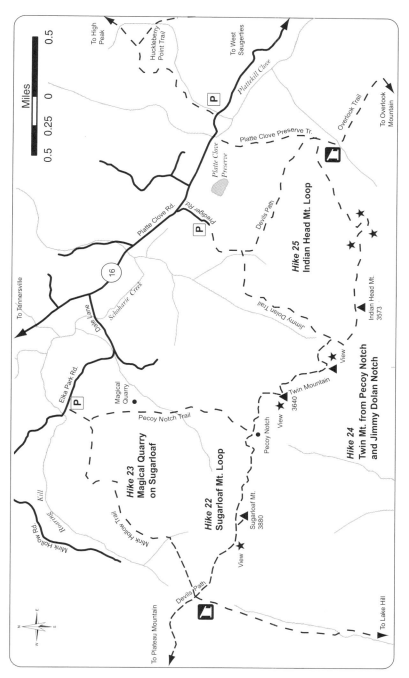

Hikes 22, 23, 24, and 25

light) to County Route 16. From Hunter, travel east on NY 23A to Bloomer Road (County Route 16), and turn right. At the junction of County Route 16 and Elka Park Road, turn left. To ascend via Pecoy Notch, continue east 2.8 mi on County Route 16 (Platte Clove Road) to Dale Lane: Turn right on Dale Lane. At a junction in 0.5 mi, bear right onto Elka Park Road, crossing a small stream, and continue for another 0.7 mi.

Via Jimmy Dolan Notch; follow the same directions but continue east past Dale Lane 1.1 mi to Prediger Road. Turn right for 0.4 mi.

The trailhead also can be approached from West Saugerties via a steep ascent up Platte Clove Mountain Road. This road is closed in winter.

Parking and trailhead: Pecoy Notch: Park in the large parking area left (just before the bridge over the Roaring Kill; worth a look, later). There is an information board at this new trailhead, with a trail register 50 ft up the trail.

Jimmy Dolan Notch: Parking space is tight along the side of Prediger Road at this beginning of the Devils Path. (Park with care. Cars that block Prediger Road, where several homes are located, have been ticketed.) Begin on the red-marked Devils Path, through the fence to the right of private property.

Pecoy Notch approach: From the parking lot, follow the yellow-marked trail to a junction at 0.3 mi. Turn left on the blue-marked trail, heading south along an old quarry road, climbing moderately. After one more steep pitch up, the trail traverses Mudd Quarry through talus. A level walk through a deciduous woods brings you to a hemlock grove. Look for trail markers, left, to descend to Dibbles Quarry at 1.0 mi, a wonderful place to explore, relax, and soak up views (see Hike 23). Beyond, crossing a good bridge, you walk high above the stream. Look for bear claw marks on the beech trees. In the meadow, good views of Twin and Sugarloaf open up.

Turn right at the old Pecoy Notch Trail beyond, and climb another 0.4 mi to Pecoy Notch. In only 0.7 mi, you'll ascend another 830 ft on one of the most rugged and spectacular sections of the Devils Path. Take a good break here, and have plenty of water.

Turn left on the red-marked Devils Path in Pecoy Notch, and begin ascending moderately. Steep ascents soon begin, including a 75-foot ascent up often precarious ledges. A short, gradual grade allows a breather and offers a lookout, right. You pass a large overhang cave, left, and squeeze between narrowly spaced boulders. In the next 0.2 mi, the trail ascends more gradually to the rock bluff that is the higher of Twin's two summits at 3640 ft. There are great views south and west.

It's worth the extra 0.6 mi hike over Twin's upper reaches to the more open ledges of the southeast summit. It involves minor loss of ascent down ledges and slight ascent to this fine open area, with different perspectives. Or hike directly to this area via Jimmy Dolan Notch, below.

Jimmy Dolan Notch approach: For the first 0.4 mi, follow the red-marked Devils Path to the junction with the Jimmy Dolan Notch Trail. Turn right here and follow blue trail markers through a shady hemlock woods. The last 0.5 mi becomes more steep and rocky as you approach the notch, where you can break before resuming the steep ascent. (The sign here, "Twin summit, 1.05 mi" refers to the true north summit, 0.6 mi farther than the south overlook, your destination.)

Turn right on the red-marked Devils Path. You soon arrive at a large overhanging ledge, left, where the trail turns right. Markers are scarce in this section. In 0.2 mi, you walk under an interesting rock overhang. For another 0.2 mi, the Devils Path offers its characteristic challenges, up very steep rock to a nice view straight across to Indian Head. After brief pitches upward, the trail levels into a sunny, spruce-lined walk to the wonderful south summit, where you emerge onto large, open lookout ledges.

On a clear day the whole southern Catskills spread out before you. Overlook Mountain, with its two towers (radio and fire), stands to the southeast and beyond is the Hudson River Valley. Cooper Lake is south. To the west, Olderbark Mountain extends south from Plateau Mountain, and Sugarloaf is the next peak west.

Look across Twin to its second and true summit more than half a mile to the northwest (offering fine views also). The trail descends gradually and ascends more steeply to the true summit.

In winter, be sure to carry full crampons and snowshoes and choose a day when the snow packs well, allowing you to make "steps" for ascending the steep ledges.

25. Indian Head Mountain Loop

Round-trip distance: 7.0 mi (11.3 km)
Elevation change: 1573 ft (480 m)
Summit elevation: 3573 ft (1089 m)
Difficulty: Difficult, with two challenging near-vertical ascents up cliffs
Maps: Page 79; Trail Conference Map 41 (O-4); USGS Kaaterskill 7.5′

Summary: Experience the picturesque beginning of the Devils Path, at first winding through level, shady hemlock woods, then beginning its ascent over Indian Head off the Old Overlook Road. Parts of the Indian Head profile involve steep sections, one extremely steep, as the summit is approached from the east. Of course, these are the areas with the magnificent views.

▶ **Access to area:** From NY 23A in Tannersville, take Depot Road south (at light) to County Route 16. From NY 23A east of Hunter, turn south on Bloomer Road (County Route 16). From the junction of County Route 16 and Elka Park Road, continue left on County Route 16 (Platte Clove Road) for 3.9 mi to Prediger Road. Turn right 0.4 mi to road's end.

The trailhead also can be approached from West Saugerties via a steep ascent up Platte Clove Mountain Road. This road is closed in winter.

Parking and trailhead: Park along the side of the road. The trail begins to the right of the private property, through a narrow opening in a log fence. ◀

You are beginning the eastern end of the Devils Path, one of the most challenging and rewarding areas for Catskill hiking. Historians say that the name Devils Path comes from old fears of the unexplored area above the Great Wall of Manitou, looming 1600 ft above the Hudson River Valley. Native Americans and European settlers alike avoided the Catskills, for behind that wall in the dark hemlock forests the Devil himself lived amongst wild animals! The Devils Tombstone Campground is 12 mi west over the Devils Path. Some hikers today say the name comes from the roller-coaster nature of the 23-mile Devils Path.

Crossing a stream on a narrow wooden bridge without a railing (harrowing in winter), the red-marked trail proceeds southwest on an old woods road. At the junction with the Jimmy Dolan Notch Trail (which you will descend), continue left on the red-marked trail through a hemlock woods on gradual grades. After a downgrade, you reach Old Overlook Road (used in colonial days) at 1.9 mi. The Devils Path curves right, but take a moment to follow the road left a few yards past a deep pit into an old quarry where people have made a rock throne and other stonework. (On a sunny day, keep an eye out for a snake enjoying the rock.)

Returning to the trail, now briefly merged with Old Overlook Road, watch for another junction soon where you turn right on the Devils Path, heading west to Indian Head. *It's easy to miss this junction,* which is located at a wider spot with logs, for the sign is in shady trees. For 0.8 mi, the ascent is through an attractive woods with many level stretches that allow you to catch your breath between pitches to higher terrain.

Steep climbing for the next 0.5 mi brings you to Shermans Lookout at the chin of the Indian. You feel that you've earned this one! The lookout offers expansive 180-degree views of the Hudson River Valley, Kaaterskill High Peak to the north, and Plattekill Mountain near to the southeast, and the ledges of Huckleberry Point across the drop. There's a fine view of Bruderhof Community buildings, north, and of Woodstock's Karma Triyana Dharmachakra Monastery below Overlook Mountain south, through binoculars.

Above Shermans Lookout, the narrow trail circles near a sharp drop to the left and up rugged rocky ledges. Then the trail changes character completely, leveling out on soft evergreen needles to a second excellent overlook south, with expansive views as far as the Burroughs Range, Peekamoose, and Table Mountains. The trek continues on the level through cool balsam and hemlock woods and even loses ascent.

Suddenly you come to a 50-foot scramble up a cut in the cliff to a third marvelous rock ledge, 0.5 mi from Shermans Lookout. At the bottom, look up; the ledge hangs over the forest like an enormous high diving board. Climbing one section of this cliff can be challenging, a real stretch for shorter legs. Otherwise, the layered rock and many tree roots assist the ascent.

From this large ledge, the section of Indian Head you just traversed is directly across, with Overlook Mountain on the right. The Ashokan Reservoir is prominent to the south. In 0.2 mi, the grade levels to another dramatic cliff. A path left takes you closer to the vertical rock wall, perhaps 50 ft high. Here, too, one area is difficult to scale without long, strong legs—or assistance. The trail goes along the cliff top for a few feet, frightening in winter!

For another 0.3 mi, the trail continues, over mostly level terrain, across the wooded summit, elevation 3573 ft. As you descend 475 ft to the col between Indian Head and Twin Mountains in 0.5 mi, consider that this is the easiest of the Devils Path descents between here and Hunter Mountain. (The descent off Twin is 830 ft in 0.8 mi; off Sugarloaf, 1200 ft in 1 mi; and from Plateau's Orchard Point to the NY 214 trailhead, 1600 ft in 1.3 mi. A path deserving of its name!)

Partway down, an opening through trees from a ledge nicely frames the Black Dome Range. Twin Mountain is near to the west. When you reach the blue-marked Jimmy Dolan Notch Trail in the col, turn right to descend to the trailhead. (Or take advantage of being at this 3100-foot col, and climb only 0.4 mi and 400+ ft to Twin Mountain's spectacular south summit ledges; see Hike 24.)

The descent from the col is steady and rocky, and requires careful attention. After 0.8 mi, your descent moderates as you climb out of the notch, and becomes a pleasant walk through a shady hemlock forest. After crossing a stream, you reach the original junction and turn left, following red markers back to the trailhead.

In winter, the very steep sections on the eastern approach to Indian Head should be avoided unless you have considerable experience with winter mountain hiking and full crampons. Over this terrain, it is essential that snow texture be packable to create stable footing. The area should be avoided when snow is light and ice prevails.

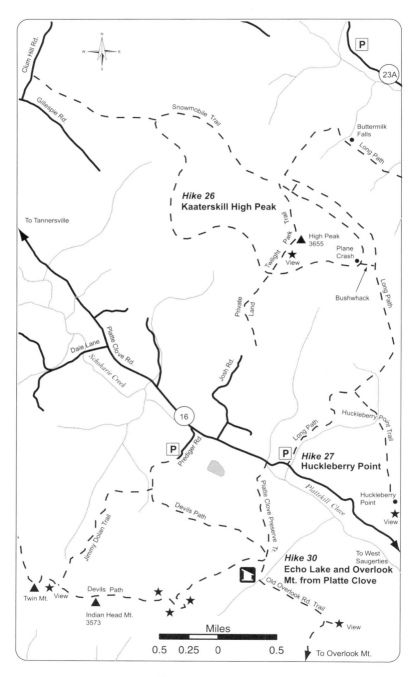

Hikes 26, 27, and 30

"If I were to name the three most precious resources of life,

I should say books, friends, and nature."

—JOHN BURROUGHS

East Catskills

The great mountains looming atop the escarpment were at one time thought to harbor wizards, witches, and even the very devil himself. People sought out a "witch doctor," Jacob Brinks, to deal with them. What a contrast with later years, when these areas were considered of unsurpassed beauty and the Catskills became "the place to be."

Until 1870, Kaaterskill High Peak was believed to be the highest mountain in the Catskills because of its prominence when viewed from the Hudson River Valley. For nearly one hundred years, hotels attracted people from the cities to Overlook Mountain in Woodstock, which offers one of the best views from a fire tower in the Catskills.

If you have time after a hike, want a change of pace, or the weather isn't cooperating, consider one of the following attractions:

Karma Triyana Dharmachaka Monastery. At Overlook Mountain trailhead, Meads Mountain Road, Woodstock. Tours, 1:30 P.M., Sat. and Sun. 845-679-3400.

Woodstock Historical Society Museum. June 15–Oct. 15, 1–5 P.M. 845-679-2256.

Tubing the Esopus Creek. Transportation is offered from Phoenicia upstream allowing you to tube the Esopus Creek past the village to the Catskill Mountain railroad, which brings you back to Phoenicia. Town Tinker, 845-688-5553, or F-S Tube Rental, 845-688-7633.

Catskill Mountain Railroad. A scenic, 6-mile round-trip rail ride along the Esopus Creek from Mountain Pleasant to Phoenicia. NY 28, Mt. Pleasant, N.Y.

Kenneth L. Wilson Campground. A public campground located off NY 28 near Boiceville. Swimming, nonmotorized boating.

Empire State Railway Museum. Phoenicia. Ulster and Delaware station with exhibits on the history of Catskill Mountain railroads. 845-688-7501.

26. Kaaterskill High Peak

Round-trip distance: 8.8 mi (14.2 km)
Elevation change: 1705 ft (520 m)
Summit elevation: 3655 ft (1114 m)
Difficulty: Strenuous
Maps: Page 84; Trail Conference Map 41 (O-4); USGS Kaaterskill 7.5'

Summary: This southern approach to Kaaterskill High Peak offers a nice mix of terrain, ranging from very steep near the summit to long level sections at 3000 ft. The forests vary from deciduous woods to shady conifer forest. Large, open ledges beyond the summit offer spectacular views.

▶ **Access to area:** From NY 23A in Tannersville, take Depot Road south (at light) to County Route 16. From NY 23A east of Hunter, turn right on Bloomer Road (County Route 16). From the junction of County Route 16 and Elka Park Road, continue left on County Route 16 (Platte Clove Road) for 5 mi (0.9 mi east of Prediger Road). The trailhead also can be approached from West Saugerties via a steep ascent up Platte Clove Mountain Road. This road is closed in winter.

Parking and trailhead: Turn north on a dirt road with a DEC sign just west of the bridge where Platte Clove Road begins to descend. (Walk to this bridge at some point to view the chasm below, known as Devils Kitchen.) Park in a large cleared area, right, a few feet up the dirt road. ◀

The road ascends steadily through a hemlock forest, with sounds of Plattekill Creek below. Bear right at a fork in 0.7 mi. Note the double trail markers, which indicate the turn. Turn right again at 0.9 mi. (Continue past the yellow-marked trail, right, which leads to breathtaking Huckleberry Point in 1.3 mi. See Hike 27.)

Continuing left on the blue-marked Long Path, you ascend an additional 800 ft to a broad, flat plateau known as Pine Plains at 3000 ft, which offers over a mile of scenic strolling through cool evergreens and, in season, blueberries. This area can be wet, so hiking is ideal after a dry period or in winter.

At 3.3 mi after a very gradual downgrade, you leave the Long Path, turning left to follow the snowmobile trail south. After a moderate climb, turn right very briefly at another junction. Watch for a rock cairn where the snowmobile trail dips to a small drainage in 0.1 mi. At this point, you turn left, following the blue trail blazes of the informally marked Twilight Park Trail to the summit. This primitive path's beginning, off the snowmobile trail, is not obvious because it crosses a wet area and blue blazes are scarce. Soon the trail improves.

Hike another 650 ft for a half mile up this rugged informal trail to the summit, sometimes ascending very steeply through rock cuts and up ledges. Behind you, looking north, views of the Blackhead Range and Stoppel Point are visible from the top of a boulder. With binoculars, you can pick out the rock ledges of North

Point. In another 0.2 mi, still ascending steadily, you reach the wooded summit. *Be sure to hike 0.3 mi farther*, descending slightly, to the magnificent open Hurricane Ledges overlooking the southern Catskills! From these sunny flat rocks, you get splendid views of the Devils Path mountains near to the south. This is a great place to enjoy a long, leisurely lunch. Retrace to the summit and descend by the same informal trail.

On your ascent, if you have good compass skills, you can bushwhack 0.2 mi west to the snowmobile trail where the Long Path levels off at 3000 ft in a hemlock forest. It's a shorter, drier, and more direct route south to the open Hurricane Ledges. (Tend northward as you head west, and bring long pants to avoid nettles.) At the snowmobile trail, turn left for a mile to a blue-marked path. Turn right and climb 500 ft, very steeply below the open ledges—your destination.

Return via the north path over the summit, turning right briefly on the snowmobile trail below, then left at the nearby junction to descend to the Long Path, where you turn right. Or retrace south, turn left on the snowmobile trail to the site of a plane wreck, where you bushwhack east to the Long Path and turn right. (Do *not* follow the blue-marked informal trail south; it enters restricted private land.)

Kaaterskill High Peak is a beautiful winter hike, but the final section up the informal Twilight Park Trail is north-facing and the steep ledges are often icy. Full crampons are essential.

27. Huckleberry Point

Round-trip distance: 4.8 mi (7.7 km)
Elevation change: 1100 ft (335 m), including ascent on return
High-point elevation: 2500 ft (762 m)
Difficulty: Moderate
Maps: Page 84; Trail Conference Map 41 (O-4); USGS Kaaterskill 7.5′

Summary: Huckleberry Point is one of the spectacular places in the Catskills. You suddenly emerge from woods full of mountain laurel to open rock ledges which drop 1000 ft to Plattekill Clove below. Plan an extensive stay on a very clear day, enjoying views of the Hudson River Valley, Overlook Mountain, and the steep slopes of Indian Head and Plattekill Mountains across the narrow clove gorge.

▶ **Access to area:** From NY 23A in Tannersville, turn south on Depot Road at light to County Route 16. From NY 23A east of Hunter, turn right on Bloomer Road (County Route 16). From the junction of County Route 16 and Elka Park Road, continue left on County Route 16 (Platte Clove Road) for 5 mi.

The trailhead also can be approached from West Saugerties via a steep ascent up Platte Clove Mountain Road. This road is closed in winter.

Parking and trailhead: Turn north on a dirt road with a DEC sign, before a bridge. (Walk to this bridge at some point to view the chasm below, known as Devils Kitchen.) Park in a large cleared area, right, a few feet up the road. ◄

The trail ascends steadily up the woods road, gaining 300 vertical feet before the first junction at 0.7 mi, where you bear right. (Note double markers, which indicate a turn.) In another 0.3 mi, the trail again takes a right turn, which is not as clearly marked. Beyond, at 1.1 mi, turn right again on the yellow-marked Huckleberry Point Trail.

From the junction, the trail very slowly loses elevation to Plattekill Creek at 0.4 mi. Piles of rocks in the woods are probably evidence of old homesteads. In most seasons, rock-hopping across the creek is no problem, but in spring, or if the weather has been excessively wet, the water can be high.

You begin ascending the ridge, climbing a few moderate ledges to a level walk through mountain laurel across the ridge top. At 0.8 mi, the trail descends steeply down the ridge's southern side. Be careful; footing can be tricky on the loose pebbles.

The trail soon becomes a delightful ramble through lovely woods, first of maple, beech, and birch, then changing character, winding through especially bountiful and tall mountain laurel under red pine and oak. The scent of pine needles on a sunny day is sublime. (If you plan your hike to see the mountain laurel blooms in June, be advised it can still be blackfly season, so choose a breezy day. You will want to stay at Huckleberry Point for a long lunch and not be hurried away by bugs.)

After passing through a stand of pine, follow the yellow-marked trail right at a T junction. (On your return, note this left turn and find yellow markers as you continue. Only partly-obscured, old red and white markers remain at the junction, and it looks like the trail continues straight ahead.)

Ahead, sky appears through the trees, and suddenly you arrive at open rocks, beyond which is a sheer drop of 1000 ft to Platte Clove. This is one of the most magnificent views in the Catskills, southeast over the Hudson River Valley region and far south to a dramatic silhouette of the Shawangunks over the Ashokan Reservoir. Overlook Mountain with its two towers rises steeply out of the valley. Just across the drop is Plattekill and Indian Head Mountains. This is the best place from which to see the distinct profile of Indian Head Mountain. The Twin Mountain summits are beyond. Enjoy a leisurely lunch, watching the vultures and ravens ride the thermals.

When you can tear yourself away from this wonderful spot, retrace and be aware of staying on the yellow-marked trail. After descending the ridge, the path seems to fork and you go left. This popular area has many informal paths, so always note markers after a turn. If you don't see any, retrace your steps.

28. Poets Ledge and Wildcat Falls

Round-trip distance: Poets Ledge, 5.2 mi (8.4 km); Wildcat Falls, 6.7 mi (10.8 km); hiking both, 7.7 mi (12.4 km). Road-walk 1.3 mi (2.1 km) additional
Elevation change: Poets Ledge, 1700 ft (518 m) (descending 300 ft (91 m) from main trail); Wildcat Falls, 1500 ft (457 m); hiking both, about 1800 ft (549 m)
High-point elevation: Poets Ledge, 1900 ft (579 m); Wildcat Falls, 2100 ft (640 m)
Difficulty: Strenuous
Maps: Page 90; Trail Conference Map 41 (O, P-4); USGS Kaaterskill 7.5'

Summary: This is a trip far up the northeast shoulder of Kaaterskill High Peak to the top of Wildcat Falls and superb views of famous Kaaterskill Clove from Poets Ledge. Be well-conditioned for this trip, for most of the climbing occurs in the first two miles, making it a steady, moderately steep ascent. The destinations make it well worth your effort. This trail is a section of the Long Path, which starts near New York City at the George Washington Bridge and is being extended to the Adirondacks.

▶ **Access to area:** From the south on NY 32A, turn left at traffic light on NY 23A in Palenville. Travel 0.6 mi to an unmarked pullout just before the "Entering Catskill Park" sign. From the west on NY 23A, travel to Palenville, then across the bridge for 0.3 mi to a pullout on left.

Parking and trailhead: Park just east of the "Entering Catskill Park" sign on NY 23A, 0.3 mi east of the bridge and west of the Palenville village sign. There is an unmarked pullout with room for several cars next to State Land signs. Walk west to the bridge, turn left, and walk 0.4 mi along Malden Avenue. Just beyond the Fernwood Restaurant is a dirt road, right, which you follow for a few feet to the trail, right, beyond a barrier. Do not continue up the dirt road. Bear right up the trail, marked by green blazes, which passes above the restaurant. ◀

Trail footing is initially rocky, but improves quickly above the switchback. Note the double green blaze as you approach a fork, meaning a direction change. Bear right at the fork, following green blazes. State Land begins at 0.5 mi. Blue DEC trail markers now guide you.

The trail continues its climb generally southwest, and as it reaches impressive rock ledges, note the double blue trail markers which signal a turn, right. As you ascend the red shale ledges, it becomes apparent why this path was once called Red Gravel Road. The trail turns north and levels out, now an attractive mossy path among mountain laurel, a welcome breather. It circles west near the clove drop off, where ravens and vultures ride the thermals. Entering hemlock woods, a path right leads some distance to a view, but a better one awaits above. Steady climbing through deciduous woods reaches picturesque mossy ledges (note rubbery "peeling paint" fungus), just before reaching a striking lookout at 1.8 mi.

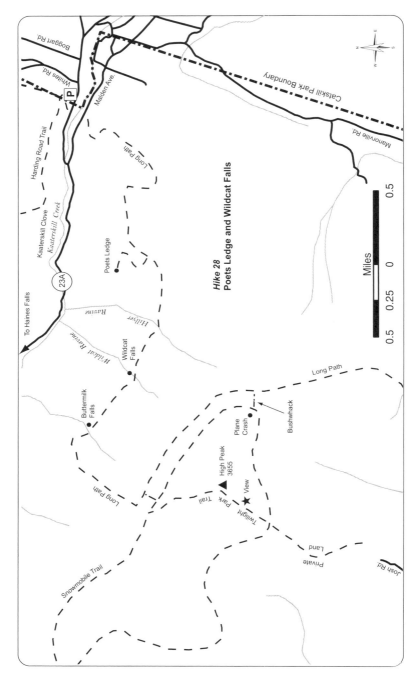

Hike 28

Poets Ledge and Wildcat Falls

Miles

0.5   0.25   0   0.5

Hike 28

The short path, right, offers a great view over Kaaterskill Clove and the northeast Hudson River Valley.

More climbing up sometimes slippery ledges brings you to a height of land where the trail levels out in an attractive older-growth hemlock forest. A little over two miles from the trailhead, a sign indicates Poets Ledge, 0.5 mi to the right off the Long Path. Do it now or later, but don't miss this very attractive trail and spectacular view of Kaaterskill Clove and surrounding mountains. Total descent to Poets Ledge is approximately 300 ft, but it occurs in different sections and the return is not difficult.

The yellow-marked Poets Ledge Trail begins on nearly level terrain, then descends slightly. After one substantial drop down a rock bluff, the trail reaches a flat-rock clearing with a fire pit. Long-needled scotch pine add to the beauty of the old-growth hemlock. You arrive at a good view north from a rock, but don't stop yet! The trail drops down through interesting ledges and heads through level woods to a superb view from an open ledge. NY 23A snakes up the gorge, Kaaterskill High Peak is near to the south, Blackhead and Black Dome Mountains rise beyond the escarpment, north.

Back at the main trail, turn right (west) to Wildcat Falls. Descending slightly, parts of the trail are wet from springs, and eroded, with exposed roots. Continue over a lovely brook that falls into Hillyer Ravine. The trail swings closer to the drop-off, then turns left up a rock ledge. Continuing west, you hear a waterfall, and at 3.4 mi arrive at Wildcat Falls, which drops out of sight below a great rock ledge you can walk out on (carefully). Though you can't see the falls, views from the ledge are superb overlooking the Hudson River Valley and Kaaterskill Clove. This is a great spot for lunch. Note the pretty falls farther upstream.

Retrace from Wildcat Falls or continue through level woods for 0.5 mi to the top of Buttermilk Falls, not easily viewed. As you approach, you can barely see part of the top falls and part of the second cataract, which plunges down the gorge out of sight. **Use extreme caution in this area.** The drop is more than 100 ft to the second section. Do **not** descend to get a better view, and remember that Catskill rock is slippery. Retrace your steps from Buttermilk Falls.

29. Overlook Mountain from Woodstock

Round-trip distance: 5.0 mi (8.1 km)
Elevation change: 1400 ft (427 m)
Summit elevation: 3140 ft (957 m)
Difficulty: Moderate; steady climb to former site of
    Overlook Mountain House, mostly easy to summit
Maps: Page 93; Trail Conference Map 41 (O-5); USGS Woodstock 7.5'

Summary: This peak is aptly named. Several states can be seen from this eastern summit on a clear day, as well as New York State landmarks like the Hudson River, the Ashokan Reservoir, Slide Mountain, and Hunter Mountain. Overlook Mountain House, a grand hotel that burned twice, adorned the mountain near its summit. The stock market crash of 1929 halted the second rebuilding. The ruins are still there, as well as a renovated fire tower. Rattlesnakes have been seen in the rocky summit area.

▶ **Access to area**: From Woodstock village, take County Route 33 north for 0.6 mi to Meads Mountain Road (crossing Glasco Turnpike). Continue north up steep, winding Meads Mountain Road for 2.1 mi to the DEC signpost.

Parking and trailhead: Park in the large parking area, right. Across the road is the former Mead's Mountain House, now the Karma Triyana Dharmachaka Monastery. The trail register is just beyond the barrier. ◀

As you start, look at the view to Indian Head Mountain from the meadow, left. Red DEC trail markers guide you steadily up an old road, the Overlook Mountain Trail, but they are not needed. Take your time up the steady ascent and enjoy mossy rock ledges and mountain laurel on the roadside. Pick a cool day or hike early, for shade is scarce on this road. Where the grade eases at a swing left, you may be ready to break and explore overhangs in the woods, right. After the next climb, a large level rock also invites a break. Bear left at a fork at 1.1 mi. The climb does not abate until the Overlook Mountain House is in sight as you swing left around the top of the ridge at 1.7 mi.

Quite a sight it is, an impressive reminder of the nineteenth-century heyday of building grand hotels in the Catskill Mountains. On April Fool's Day in 1874, a child tried in vain to convince people that the chimney smoke was darker than usual; Overlook Mountain House burned to the ground. Now, a spiral staircase inside ascends into thin air. Pictures of the building are on many walls. One reads: "The Overlook Mountain House, on the highest point of the Catskill range, was opened June 15, 1871. All modern conveniences, including Gas and Telegraph facilities. Reached by boat or Rail to Rondout; Rondout and Oswego Railroad to West Hurley [9 mi]; thence by the Hotel Stages in 3 hours."

This landmark was indeed the highest of all the great hotels. A favorite pastime for guests, it is said, was to push boulders off the cliffs of the escarpment, for the fun of seeing them crash far below! A large antenna is near a small building dated 1928, the year before the rebuilding was halted when the stock market crashed. Old foundations surround the area, including a small one with a rocky ledge intruded into it for some mysterious purpose.

At 1.9 mi, you reach the junction with the Old Overlook Road Trail. Bear right onto the spur trail, which heads east and gradually climbs to superb vistas from several open ledges. In winter, this path is closed, perhaps because it goes right to

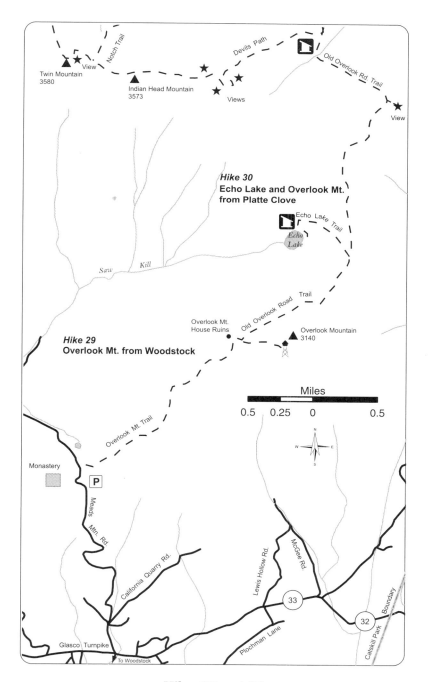

Twin Mountain
3580

Notch Trail

View

Devils Path

Old Overlook Rd. Trail

Indian Head Mountain
3573

Views

View

Hike 30
Echo Lake and Overlook Mt.
from Platte Clove

Echo Lake Trail

Echo Lake

Saw   *Kill*

Old Overlook Road   Trail

Overlook Mt.
House Ruins

Overlook Mountain
3140

Hike 29
Overlook Mt. from Woodstock

Overlook Mt. Trail

Miles

0.5   0.25   0   0.5

N
W   E
S

Monastery

P

Meads

Mtn. Rd.

California Quarry Rd.

Lewis Hollow Rd.

McGee Rd.

33

Plochman Lane

32

Catskill Park Boundary

Glasco Turnpike

To Woodstock

Hikes 29 and 30

the edge. **Keep children in tow.** Follow the path to the broad open rock, where it turns left toward the fire tower. In winter, you follow the road straight to the summit.

A fire observer's cabin, picnic tables, and the renovated fire tower are on the summit, which offers magnificent vistas of Indian Head Mountain and Kaaterskill High Peak near to the north, with the Blackhead Range behind; Twin, Sugarloaf, Plateau, and Hunter Mountains to the northwest along the Devils Path; and Ashokan Reservoir and Ashokan High Point to the southwest. Slide Mountain is far to the west, and on a clear day, the Overlook summit also offers sweeping vistas east past the Hudson to New England mountains. On weekends, volunteers at the tower answer your questions and sell merchandise. **Beware of rattlesnakes,** which can be found on and under ledges here.

Retracing your steps from the summit, turn left at the junction with the Old Overlook Road Trail.

Consider an additional trek to Echo Lake, the only natural lake in a designated wilderness area in the Catskills. Note, however, that this side trip necessitates an 850-foot descent from the junction and an additional 2.0 mi, one way. The trail heads northeast down Old Overlook Road Trail (see Hike 30), a scenic gradual descent. You'll pass an interesting balanced rock, and a spring 0.4 mi farther. Where the trail turns north, you descend on varying grades to the Echo Lake junction. The rocky old road, which led to the last Native American encampment in the Catskills, descends 455 ft to the lake and lean-to in 0.6 mi.

Retrace from Echo Lake, turning right at junctions, to descend to the parking area.

30. Echo Lake and Overlook Mountain from Platte Clove

Round-trip distance: Echo Lake, 8.0 mi (12.9 km); Overlook Mountain,
     10.6 mi (17.1 km); both, 11.8 mi (19 km)
Elevation change: Echo Lake, 1255 ft (383 m); Overlook Mountain,
     1340 ft (409 m); both, 1795 ft (547 m)
Summit elevation: 3140 ft (957 m)
Difficulty: Echo Lake: Moderately easy; a long trek on easy grades, descending
     455 ft to lake. Overlook Mountain: Moderate. Both: Moderate, but long.
Maps: Pages 84 and 93; Trail Conference Map 41 (O-4);
     USGS Kaaterskill 7.5' and Woodstock 7.5'

Summary: A delightful walk featuring stone quarries with seats and benches, a mountain brook by a lean-to, a glorious lookout to the Hudson River Valley, and mountain laurel. Descend 455 ft to Echo Lake, a stronghold of the Native Americans in the Revolutionary War, and the only natural lake in a designated wilderness area in the Catskills. The gradual grades of Old Overlook Road (now a trail) make this a great snowshoe or ski.

▶ **Access to area:** From NY 23A in Tannersville, take County Route 16 south. From NY 23A east of Hunter, turn south on Bloomer Road (County Route 16). From the junction of County Route 16 (Platte Clove Road) and Elka Park Road, continue left on County Route 16 for 4.8 mi. From West Saugerties, up Platte Clove Mountain Road, which is closed in winter: Turn north on a dirt road marked by a DEC sign.

Parking and trailhead: The parking area is a few feet up the dirt road. Walk 0.2 mi west on Platte Clove Road, just beyond a red cabin, to the Platte Clove Preserve sign on the south (left) side of the road. The trail drops down a bank 30 ft to Platte-kill Creek. Follow green Platte Clove Preserve arrows (not the blue markers). ◀

Note the beautiful waterfall and pool to the left before crossing Plattekill Creek on an impressive new bridge with a dedication to the events of September 11, 2001. The trail gradually ascends through a shady hemlock forest following green Platte Clove Preserve markers. This section of trail is also part of the Long Path. In 1.0 mi, look for a deep notch in the rock, left, and follow a path into the quarry which features rock benches with worked stone slabs, a large stone throne, and a nearly camouflaged little chair, a fine place to break.

Back on the trail, the red-marked Devils Path soon enters from the right. At another junction where the Devils Path turns right toward Indian Head Mountain, you continue straight ahead on the blue-marked Old Overlook Road Trail.

The Devils Kitchen lean-to is situated 40 ft above a lovely rushing brook, the Cold Kill. A log bridge crosses over its cascades.

After ascending rocky trail for 0.7 mi, watch carefully for a spur path, left, with yellow markers that curves through mountain laurel to a magical spot in a large stone quarry. A stone bench overlooks the Hudson River Valley. Birches grow out of the steep rocky slope below. Here is the perfect spot to break. Explore this extensive area.

Retracing, the now-level Old Overlook Road Trail is very attractive, with excellent footing and bountiful mountain laurel. The trail contours the slope for over a mile below Plattekill Mountain. Views of Overlook Mountain open up ahead, especially when leaves are off the trees. A spur path leads to a campsite.

At 3.3 mi, turn right on the yellow-marked Echo Lake Trail and descend a surprising 455 ft (a gradual, rocky descent) for 0.6 mi to the Echo Lake lean-to. Located in tall trees in open woods, the lean-to is set across the lake from Overlook Mountain. Paths lead in both directions to other camping sites. From the other side of Echo Lake, Plattekill's ledges stand out. Ducks of different varieties abound here.

If you wish to extend the hike to Overlook Mountain, which has a fire tower and superb views in all directions, it is 1.9 mi and an additional 600-foot ascent beyond the Echo Lake junction to the summit. There are views of Indian Head Mountain as you ascend this old road, especially good views in late fall and winter. The summit is 0.5 mi from the junction with the Overlook Mountain Trail. Follow the path beyond to the right; it climbs to superb vistas from many open ledges. **Beware of rattlesnakes**, which can be found on and under the ledges.

31. Mount Tremper from Willow

Round-trip distance: 8.0 mi (12.9 km); traverse over mountain to Phoenicia
    trailhead, 7.0 mi (11.3 km)
Elevation change: 1640 ft (500 m)
Summit elevation: 2740 ft (835 m)
Difficulty: Moderately strenuous
Maps: Page 97; Trail Conference Map 41 (M-5); USGS Bearsville 7.5'
    and Phoenicia 7.5'

Summary: This approach offers interesting and varied terrain while traversing a hollow and crossing a ridge to a broad summit and fire tower. Mountain laurel is plentiful in June.

➤ **Access to area:** From NY 28, turn north on NY 212 at Mount Tremper for about 3 mi to the hamlet of Willow. Turn west on Van Wagner Road for 0.4 mi. Turn left and drive to the end of Jessup Road.

Parking and trailhead: There is no parking area. Landowners are willing to share their parking area, but ask permission. Please be careful not to block their access. If full, parking would be farther back on Jessup Road. Climb 0.2 mi beyond a private road sign at the end of Jessup Road to a DEC sign, which indicates 3.6 mi to Mount Tremper's summit. It is actually 3.8 mi to the fire tower from this junction. ◀

Bear left at the DEC sign and climb steadily up the curving road. When the road swings right, the grade becomes gradual and mountain laurel grows in profusion. After a short ascent, the trail enters State Land. Mount Tobias is behind you. There are fire pits in a level woods left. You begin climbing moderately up the side of the mountain, getting closer to the dramatic rock ledges above as you ascend. The terrain drops off more steeply to the right as the trail levels and stays on contour at 2100 ft around the mountainside.

In leafless seasons, you begin to see Indian Head Mountain and part of Twin

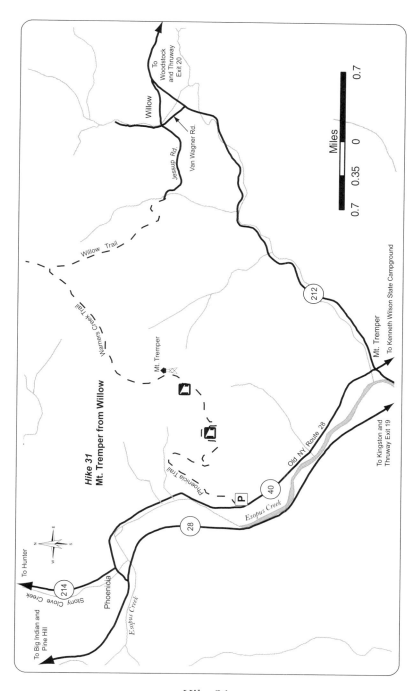

Hike 31
Mt. Tremper from Willow

Miles
0.7 0.35 0 0.7

Hike 31

Mountain to the right of Little Rocky and Olderbark Mountains in the foreground, as the wall of the hollow drops off sharply. You lose ascent angling
toward Carl Mountain, then ascend steadily to a junction at the end of Hoyts
Hollow at 1.8 mi. Turn left up a steep pitch toward Mount Tremper (trail right
heads to Warners Creek, on a new section of the Long Path). The actual distance
to the fire tower from this junction is 2.2 mi, not 1.6 mi as the sign shows. You
climb about 100 vertical feet before the trail levels and stays generally on contour
at 2500 ft, with terrain steepening above you and dropping off to the right.

The trail loses some ascent to a flat woods ridge toward Mount Tremper, then
climbs at times steeply up picturesque rocky terrain for 300+ vertical feet to the
summit ridge. Note that rattlesnakes have been seen on Mt. Tremper. You may
catch a view of Overlook Mountain and Cooper Lake. The trail swings left below
dramatic ledges, then continues on the level for another 0.4 mi to the renovated
fire tower. The area has a picnic table and lean-to. From the fire tower, views are
expansive, to the nearby Burroughs Range, Ashokan Reservoir, and the Devils Path
Mountains, with Black Dome and Blackhead visible beyond through Stony Clove.

This is a nice late October, winter, or April hike, when views are unobstructed
by foliage.

If you can spot a car at the trailhead 1.7 mi east of Phoenicia on County Route
40 (old NY 28), a fine day's trek can be made over Mount Tremper's summit,
descending on the Phoenicia Trail. The end-to-end distance of this traverse is
7.0 mi. The driving distance between the trailheads is 7.7 mi.

32. Onteora Lake

Round-trip distance: 2.8 mi (4.5 km)
Elevation change: Minor ups and downs
Difficulty: Easy
Maps: Page 99; USGS Kingston West Quad 7.5'

Summary: Native Americans are said to have called the Catskill Mountain region
Onteora, which means "land in the sky." A long loop trail proceeds along
Onteora Lake to an old bluestone mining area, through evergreen forest to a
pond, by an automobile graveyard, and through wetlands. The lake, part of the
3,000-acre Bluestone Wild Forest, offers fishing, boating, and informal campsites.

▶ **Access to area:** From NY 28, 3.0 mi west of the Kingston Thruway exit, turn
north at the Onteora Lake sign at the east end of the mini-mall. From the west
on NY 28, proceed 1.7 mi beyond the West Hurley traffic light; turn north at the
Onteora Lake sign at the east end of the mini-mall.

Parking and trailhead: Follow the access road to a large parking area near the

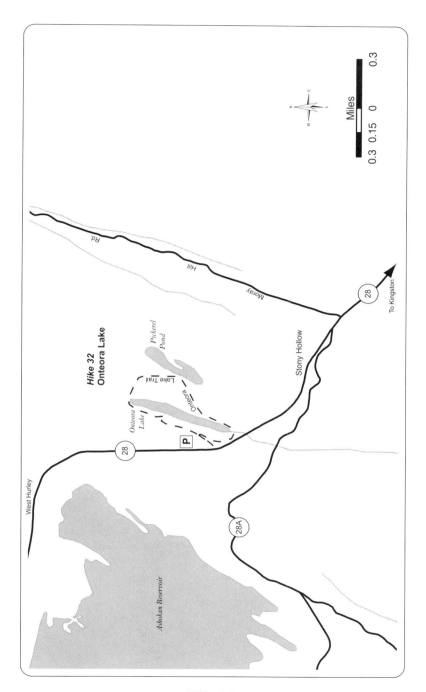

Hike 32
Onteora Lake

Pickerel
Pond

Lake Trail

Onteora

Onteora
Lake

Ashokan Reservoir

West Hurley

28

P

28A

Stony Hollow

Moray

Hill

Rd

28

To Kingston

Miles

0.3   0.15   0   0.3

Hike 32

lake. The trail begins at the information board. ◀

The trail passes between the lake and camping areas under rock ledges, a popular area. Be aware that a variety of snakes, some poisonous, exist in the Hudson River Valley Region and favor rock outcrops. The trail ascends gently, a grassy lane through pretty long-needled pine. At each of the two forks in the path, turn right.

You feel as if you're getting away from civilization, entering a shady, older-growth hemlock forest amidst rock walls, sometimes walking on bedrock. This was the old bluestone mining area. An old foundation in the woods is evidence of past enterprise, as the trail swings left. (A side path climbs over quarry piles and in 0.3 mi passes overhanging ledges. In half a mile, this informal path connects to a lane heading back, left, to your original trail, offering an alternative loop.)

Bluestone mined in this area was shipped around the world from Kingston. Catskill bluestones and sedimentary shales were formed as thousands of feet of sediments were laid down in the shallow sea that covered this region. Then a tectonic collision created the Appalachian Plateau and Catskill Delta. Erosion gouged out valleys, creating the mountains we see today.

Continuing on the marked trail, the path soon begins to ascend. Continue straight ahead where a path diverges left. Soon after descending next to a rock wall, you come upon an upside-down car, an unlikely sight. Just after the car, note that the marked trail turns right; the bike path continues straight.

The trail meanders for 0.5 mi on stony footing to Pickerel Pond. Note the turn left at a T intersection, following yellow markers. When the trail swings left between mounds, a pond appears ahead and the trail descends steadily to its shore. This area attracts a wide variety of birds. Have a snack and sit quietly. We saw pileated woodpeckers, a blue heron, and ducks. We saw wild turkeys in several places along the way. Look for salamanders in the shallows. After ascending gradually above the pond, be alert for a turn right.

Emerging from a shady hemlock woods, a very steep, short ascent at 1.9 mi brings Onteora Lake into view. The route follows the edge of a steep bank. Large rock outcrops add interest to the landscape. At 2.5 mi, the trail leads up through a cleft in the rock, arriving at the loop junction at 2.6 mi. Turn L to return. A longer excursion can be had by including the red loop or the red and blue loops.

33. Ashokan Reservoir

Round-trip distance: 2.5 mi (4 km)
Elevation change: Level terrain
Difficulty: Easy
Maps: Page 102; USGS Ashokan 7.5'

Summary: A splendid place to bike, hike, run, roller-blade, take the baby for a stroll, practice on training wheels, or otherwise get exercise surrounded by mountains, lake, and sky. This is a paved trail.

▶ **Access to area:** Traveling from Kingston on NY 28, turn left onto NY 28A at Stony Hollow. Travel about 8.0 mi and turn right on a road marked "Dead End," following it briefly to the reservoir. From the west on NY 28, turn south in Shokan on Reservoir Road for about 2.0 mi to the reservoir, and cross the causeway.

Parking and trailhead: Coming from NY 28A, park at the end of the road marked "Dead End." From NY 28, cross the causeway and turn left at the T intersection; travel below the reservoir to the road, left, marked "Dead End." The parking area at the end of this road is referred to as "the frying pan," owing to its shape. ◀

Walking westward on macadam, you see a fine view of Indian Head, Twin, and Sugarloaf Mountains in the distance across the reservoir. Ahead are Wittenberg, Cornell, Friday, Balsam Cap, Rocky, and Lone Mountains, with the highest Catskill peak, Slide Mountain, in the background. Ashokan High Point and its eastern ridge rise to the left. At the top of that east ridge is an open cobble with 270-degree views. (See Hike 46.)

Imagine this huge body of water as a tranquil rural valley dotted with villages in the first decade of the twentieth century. A crew of 400 men had removed 2,000 trees per week over a 13-square-mile area. Even cemeteries had to be moved. On September 9, 1913, a 12-mile long reservoir, up to 190 ft deep and covering more than 8,000 acres, began filling this idyllic valley. Eighty percent of the people who lived in a dozen evacuated villages remained in the region, building anew. Some moved to Kingston. Few people were paid more than a fraction of the value of their property.

The Ashokan Reservoir was the first such body of water to be built in the Catskills to provide New York City with fresh water. Ninety-two miles of tunnels transport Ashokan's water to New York City, whose citizens are taxed for the use of this resource. Several Catskill reservoirs provide fresh water fishing, boating, and viewing platforms or a walkway like the one found at Ashokan Reservoir. The reservoir is a picturesque sight, viewed from the summits of the surrounding peaks, especially from Wittenberg. (See Hike 43.)

Returning eastward, it is fun to watch Indian Head, Twin, and Sugarloaf Mountains progressively come into view. They are three of the six peaks, all over

3500 ft, that form the Devils Path, one of the Catskill's great trails, which ascends a total of 7,275 ft in 23.2 mi. (See Devils Path section.)

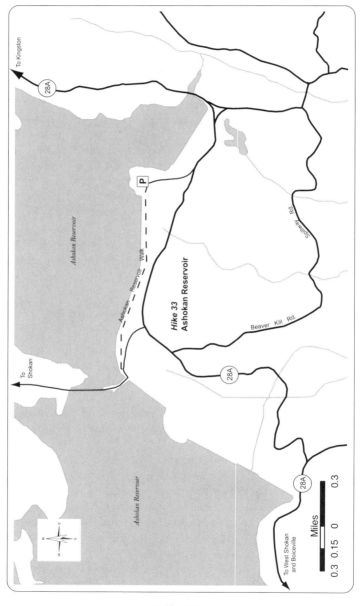

Hike 33

"To find out what you are not looking for,

to catch the shy winks and gestures on every side,

to see all the by-play going on around you,

missing no significant note or movement. . .

that is to be an observer."

—JOHN BURROUGHS

Central Catskills

This region has become a popular destination, with many resorts, fine restaurants, winter sports, cultural events, and one of the few remaining train excursions. The Catskill Center for Conservation and Development is located in Arkville. Hiking trails abound over the area's ridges and mountains, up the hollows and brooks. You may not meet anyone on some of these treks, which are far off the beaten track, yet near many popular attractions.

If you have time after a hike, want a change of pace, or the weather isn't cooperating, consider one of the following attractions:

Belleayre Mountain. Highmount, NY 28. Owned and operated by New York State Department of Environmental Conservation, Belleayre Mountain may be best known as a ski center, but it offers year-round recreation. The Sky Ride operates on weekends and holidays, and there is a train and trolley. The Belleayre Conservatory presents the Belleayre Music Festival from early July to late August. 800-942-6904; www.belleayre.com; www.belleayremusic.org.

Belleayre Beach and Pine Hill Day-Use Area. From NY 28 just east of Pine Hill, turn south under a covered bridge. Includes Pine Hill Lake, a 6-acre artificial lake with a swimming area, fishing, and picnic facilities. A very steep trail with precarious footing ascends to Belleayre. See Hike 34 for other approaches to the summit.

Delaware and Ulster Rail Ride. Arkville, NY 28. Train ride from Arkville, north to Roxbury or east to Highmount. 800-225-4132.

Catskill Center for Conservation and Development. NY 28, Arkville NY, 12406. Environmental education, arts and cultural programming, natural resource and land conservation, community planning. Workshops and lectures on Catskill region. Artists' retreat, gallery. 845-586-2611.

34. Belleayre Mountain

Round-trip distance: from Pine Hill, 6.6 mi (10.6 km);
    from Overlook Lodge, 3.4 mi (5.5 km)
Elevation change: from Pine Hill, 1325 ft (404 m);
    from Overlook Lodge, 920 ft (281 m)
Summit elevation: East Summit, 3375 ft (1029 m); true summit, 3420 ft (1043 m)
Difficulty: from Pine Hill, strenuous; from Overlook Lodge, moderate
Maps: Page 105. From Pine Hill to summit: Trail Conference Map 42
    (I-4); USGS West Kill 7.5′, Shandaken 7.5′, and Seager 7.5′.
    From Overlook Lodge to summit: Trail Conference Map 42 (H-4);
    USGS Fleischmanns 7.5′ and Seager 7.5′.

Summary: An ascent from Pine Hill to Sunset Lodge at Belleayre Mountain's summit, and a shorter, less rigorous loop hike to Sunset Lodge, beginning at Belleayre's Overlook Lodge and including the new High Peaks Interpretive Trail.
    ▶ **Access to area:** From NY 28 in Pine Hill, proceed south on Elm Street, turning right on Main Street. Turn left on Bonnie View Avenue and take the next left onto Mill Street. Continue under the trestle and up Woodchuck Hollow Road for 0.5 mi.
    From Overlook Lodge: Enter Belleayre Mountain Ski Center from NY 28 in Highmount. Drive south on County Route 49A for 1 mi and turn left to Overlook Lodge.
    Parking and trailhead: Woodchuck Hollow Road approach: At end of road, park in space to the right. Walk around the gate.
    Overlook Lodge approach: Park near first building on right (in summer an office, in winter a nursery). Ascend the macadam road past that building and turn left up a service road, which becomes the Deer Run ski trail. ◀

Pine Hill to Summit. The trail enters a shady hollow past the gate and soon makes a sharp turn east.
    An enormous boulder with overhanging ledges adorns a nearly level section before the trail swings south and ascends again. At a wet spot across the trail, note the rock wall, right, where a spring emerges and fills a rock pool. It's an interesting place to explore and catch your breath.
    Soon the trail moderates, continuing to ascend steadily but more gradually up the grassy lane through attractive open woods and sloping terrain. This is a great snowshoe trip that offers continuous views of neighboring peaks through leafless trees. At 2.0 mi, Lost Clove Trail descends east to Lost Clove Road near Big Indian.
    From this junction, the trail ascends 200 ft to the Belleayre Mountain lean-to at 2.2 mi, a fine spot to break. The next 0.2 mi is even steeper climbing, but the trail becomes gradual as it swings left through moss-covered rocky terrain toward the East Summit. A grassy glade with a flat rock offered a fire tower and great

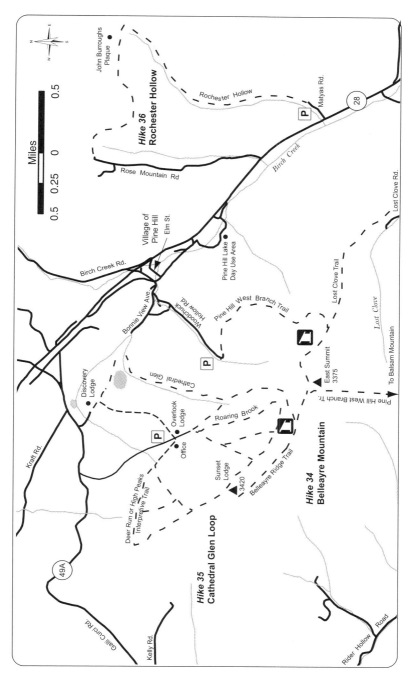

Hikes 34, 35, and 36

views for guests at area hotels decades ago. Without the tower, the only view is from the ski lodge area.

Turn west, following the red-marked Belleayre Ridge Trail for 1.0 mi to Sunset Lodge, the true summit of Belleayre Mountain. Beautiful views of the northern Catskills spread out before you atop the steep slopes. From the back deck of the lodge, look for the newly renovated fire tower on Balsam Lake Mountain, due south. With binoculars, you can see an old tower on Graham Mountain, east of Balsam Lake Mountain.

To descend, retrace to the east summit via the red-marked trail, turn left on the blue-marked Pine Hill–West Branch Trail and left at the next junction, returning the way you came.

If you can spot a second car at Overlook Lodge, walk east from Sunset Lodge to the broad, gradual slope of Roaring Brook ski trail, following it down past the pond to Overlook Lodge.

High Peaks Interpretive Trail from Overlook Lodge. The ascent via the High Peaks Interpretive Trail from Overlook Lodge is gradual at first, passing the #8 ski lift. The High Peaks Interpretive Trail, which is also called the Deer Run ski trail, has information stations about the animals, geology, trees, and history of this area.

An information kiosk is on the corner of a road turning left. Turn left up that road to read two more kiosks, one about birds of the Catskill region and a second about an old hotel site across from Belleayre Mt. If you follow this route, continue until the road ends and follow an open ski trail, right, up the mountain to Sunset Lodge on the summit. Relax on the south-facing back deck, where Balsam Lake Mt. is due south. The fire tower on its summit is renovated and open to the public. (See Hike 50, Balsam Lake Mt. Loop.)

To descend, retrace your steps east to the broad, gradual slope of Roaring Brook ski trail, following it down to Overlook Lodge.

35. Cathedral Glen Loop

Round-trip distance: 2.6 mi (4.2 km)
Elevation change: 700 ft (213 m)
Difficulty: Moderately easy
Maps: Page 105; Trail Conference Map 42 (I-4); USGS West Kill 7.5'
    and Fleischmanns 7.5'

Summary: The Cathedral Glen Loop trail descends 700 ft into a beautiful glen through old-growth hemlock forest to Belleayre Mountain's snowmaking reservoir and returns through the ski complex.

▶ **Access to area:** From NY 28 in Highmount, turn into Belleayre Mountain Ski Center (County Route 49A) for 1.0 mi, turning left to Overlook Lodge.

Parking and trailhead: Park near the lodge, walk into the ski area and continue east along a service road below the fenced pond. Cross a ski slope to a sign for, "Super Chief" and "Roaring Brook." Continue straight 0.2 mi on a service road that ends at the base of a ski slope, where another sign says "Roaring Brook" and "Discovery Lodge." Walk left across the grass to the Cathedral Glen Trail. ◀

The blue-marked DEC trail enters the woods and descends steadily on what was once an old road. Eventually, the grade moderates and becomes nearly level for long sections on good footing.

The trail descends into increasingly lovely old-growth hemlock forest, still remaining high above Cathedral Brook. About 0.8 mi down, at a rightward curve, keep a sharp eye out for an old path heading left. Follow it and it will take you to the brook, a nice diversion on a hot day.

One mile from the trail's beginning, the deep-green Belleayre snowmaking reservoir comes into view below. At its end, locate a short path left toward a large rock ledge and the reservoir, descending a mossy path to the outlet embankment. Cross on top of the embankment. (Avoid the railroad bed; legal access along the railroad is not available, despite signs and markers that suggest otherwise.)

Climb the gravel road beyond the embankment to the left, which merges into the HH ski trail. Continue uphill on HH, in summer a service road, heading west to Discovery Lodge. Leaving the woods at 1.7 mi from the beginning of the Cathedral Glen Trail, ascend below ski lifts 1 and 2 up the slope (forking left to a more gradual ascent halfway up) to Overlook Lodge parking area.

On a hot day, you may wish to reascend Cathedral Glen the way you came. The total distance is about 3.0 mi round-trip and an equal ascent, either way.

To hike this loop in reverse, walk the service road from the garages, left, near Overlook Lodge. The road becomes the "Mohican" and "Easy In" ski trails down to lifts 1 and 2 at Discovery Lodge. Turn right into the woods and bear left on the HH ski trail, following the service road down to the reservoir. Cross the embankment and ascend to the Cathedral Glen Trail, turning right on the blue-marked trail. Cross the base of the ski slope and follow the dirt road, continuing straight ahead across the ski trail to Overlook Lodge.

36. Rochester Hollow

Round-trip distance: John Burroughs' plaque, 3.5 mi (5.6 km);
   old estate foundation, 4.6 mi (7.4 km)
Elevation change: 850 ft (259 m)
Difficulty: Moderate
Maps: Page 105; Trail Conference Map 42 (I-5); USGS Shandaken 7.5' and West
Kill 7.5'

Summary: This old woods road features a plaque to naturalist John Burroughs
and the remnants of an estate in an attractive hollow in the Shandaken-Pine Hill
Wild Forest.

▶ **Access to area:** From NY 28, 1.0 mi west of the Big Indian intersection of NY
28 and County Route 47, turn north on Matyas Road.

Parking and trailhead: Continue for over 0.1 mi to a parking area at a gate.
Between the parking place and the stream, an old stone-lined opening in the
ground is interesting, but might be a hazard to small children.◀

The meandering creek near the parking area might offer good wading. Walk
around the gate and follow the lane north. In about 0.2 mi, a designated campsite to the left offers a fire pit, level ground, and the sound of the stream cascading down the hollow. Gradually ascending through open woods, you begin to
enter the characteristic hollow terrain. Hemlock now shades the lane and covers
the steep ridge rising across the stream.

You pass through stone pillars where an opening is crafted through the
stonework for runoff. The climbing steepens to 1.7 mi., and then becomes gradual where the lane curves around the hillside at the stream's origin. Soon, stone
steps lead to a plaque dedicated to John Burroughs:

   John Burroughs' Forest, April 18, 1921
   Memorial to the beloved naturalist, author, American of Slabsides
   [his Catskill retreat in West Park] and the world. Reforested by his
   neighbors, the boys of the Raymond Gordon School, and to be given
   their perpetual, joyous care under the direction of New York State
   Conservation Commission.

(For more on John Burroughs, see the opening pages of the South Catskills and
Northwest Catskills sections.)

In 0.6 mi of mostly level walking, you reach a large curving wall and stone
foundation of an old estate. (The lane continues 0.5 mi farther on a slight downgrade to a barrier at private property.) Retrace your steps for the return.

37. Rider Hollow Trail and Balsam Mountain Loop

Round-trip distance: Rider Hollow, 2.0 mi (3.2 km);
　Balsam Mountain Loop, 5.2 mi (8.4 km)
Elevation change: Rider Hollow, very little; Balsam Mountain Loop, 1600 ft (488 m)
Summit elevation: Balsam Mountain, 3600 ft (1098 m)
Difficulty: Rider Hollow, easy; Balsam Mountain Loop, strenuous
Maps: Page110; Trail Conference Map 42 (H-5);
　USGS Seager 7.5' and Shandaken 7.5'

Summary: The following trail description is in two parts. Rider Hollow is a beautiful mile along a cascading mountain brook—an ideal excursion for the whole family on a hot summer day. The Balsam Mountain Loop offers a strenuous half-day trek beyond the hollow over Balsam Mountain's summit, descending via Mine Hollow and returning to your starting point.

▶ **Access to area:** From the west on NY 28 in Arkville, turn south on Dry Brook Rd (County Route 49) immediately west of Dry Brook Bridge. In 4.7 mi, over a bridge at the Mapledale M. E. Church, turn left immediately on County Route 49A (poorly marked). In 0.5 mi, turn right on Rider Hollow Road for 2.6 mi, which becomes a narrow dirt road. From the east on NY 28, turn south on County Route 49A at Belleayre Ski Center for about 5 mi (49A becomes Todd Mountain Road) to Rider Hollow Road. Turn left.

　Parking and trailhead: Park in the DEC parking area at road's end. A trail register is at the left end of the parking area. ◀

This mile along Rider Hollow Brook is one of the most scenic brook trails in the Catskill Forest Preserve. Some hikers may wish that it offered a few more bridges, because at least four crossings are on rocks, which are not always dry or stable. Choose a low-water season, avoiding spring run-off or periods where there has been a lot of rain. However, these crossings are part of the fun. Just remember that Catskill rocks are slippery sedimentary rocks, so test them before putting your full weight on them. People try to make rock bridges, but they do not always provide stable footing. Bring wading sandals or sneakers.

　Follow red trail markers along the south bank of the brook. The trail crosses the brook on a bridge. At 0.2 mi, a new route ascends well above the brook, bypassing severe trail damage caused by Tropical Storm Irene in 2011. (For a look at the blowdown, continue straight briefly, then retrace to the new marked route). A fork, right, descends to a bridge over Rider Hollow Brook at 0.3 mi. (The yellow-marked Mine Hollow Trail, left, climbs 800 ft to the Pine Hill-West Branch Trail between Balsam and Belleayre Mountains. This will be your return route if you are ascending Balsam Mountain Loop.)

　Continue left **after** the bridge crossing for 0.2 mi to the Rider Hollow lean-to,

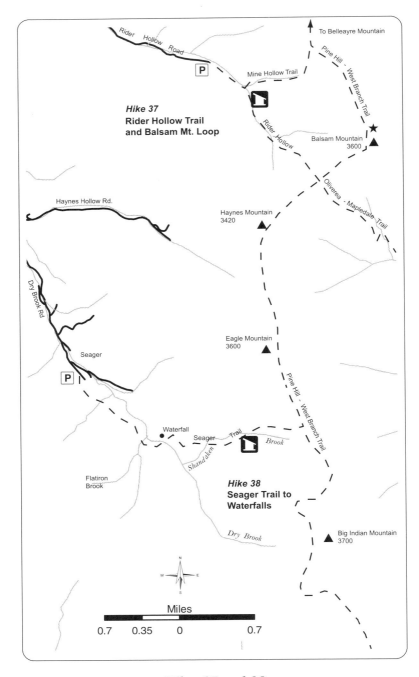

Rider Hollow Road

P

Mine Hollow Trail

Pine Hill - West Branch Trail

To Belleayre Mountain

Hike 37
Rider Hollow Trail
and Balsam Mt. Loop

Rider Hollow

★

Balsam Mountain
3600

Oliverea - Mapledale Trail

Haynes Hollow Rd.

Haynes Mountain
3420

Dry Brook Rd

Seager

P

Eagle Mountain
3600

Waterfall

Seager Trail

Brook

Shandaken

Pine Hill - West Branch Trail

Flatiron
Brook

Hike 38
Seager Trail to
Waterfalls

Dry Brook

Big Indian Mountain
3700

N
W   E
S

Miles

0.7   0.35   0   0.7

Hikes 37 and 38

set in a clearing near the brook. Just beyond, the most challenging crossing awaits, on wobbly, slippery rocks. A scenic, gradual climb takes you high above the brook and soon levels out. The trail reaches a smaller crossing and then a third one, remaining near the pools and cascades, a fine place to be on a very hot summer day.

This is the spot to turn around, for after this last crossing, the trail begins a relentless ascent of 750 vertical feet in just 0.8 mi to the Pine Hill–West Branch Trail (also known as the Biscuit Brook–Pine Hill Trail) between Balsam and Haynes Mountains. Those climbing the Balsam Mountain Loop should have long pants to protect against stinging nettles. Part way up, enjoy a break at a big rock in a shady hemlock grove. When you pass a 10-foot rock ledge, below which may be a spring, you are close to the junction at 1.8 mi.

Turn left on the blue trail. The final 550-foot climb to the summit at 2.5 mi is on gradual or moderate grades with a few steep pitches up picturesque rock ledges. Passing to the left of one jumble of rock outcrops, you can imagine fine bear caves. Miniature evergreen woods grow on one boulder; sedimentary-layered rocks jut vertically from the ground. The true summit is at this south side of Balsam's flat top. Continue north along the ridge for 0.1 mi, losing ascent slightly, to an excellent boulder overlook to Sherrill Mountain and North Dome, Hunter and Plateau, Blackhead and Black Dome far north. Way below is the hamlet of Big Indian. This view is best when leaves are off the trees.

For another 0.2 mi along the level summit, enjoy the attractive woods and spruce-filled meadow at the north end. Just beyond, the trail drops through a steep rock cut and begins its 800-foot descent to the Mine Hollow Trail junction. For 1.0 mi, the trail descends moderately or steeply through moss-covered ledges and fern-filled woods. Take care while descending the steeper pitches. After a slight upgrade, watch for the yellow-marked Mine Hollow Trail, where you turn left.

This is an attractive trail, descending through an enormous rocky outcrop and then steeply down into the hollow, winding through a hemlock grove. Emerging again into deciduous woods, the grade moderates and follows the north bank of Mine Hollow Brook to rejoin the Rider Hollow Trail at the bridge. Retrace, right, 0.4 mi to the trailhead.

38. Seager Trail to Waterfalls

Round-trip distance: 1.8 mi (2.9 km); lean-to, 4.4 mi (7.1 km)
Elevation change: 175 ft (53 m); lean-to, 500 ft (152 m)
Difficulty: Easy
Maps: Page 110; Trail Conference Map 42 (H-6); USGS Seager 7.5′

Summary: This remote trail offers a short meander next to a brook and leads to attractive waterfalls. Crossings of waterways and tributaries on rocks make this a dry-period hike.

▶ **Access to area:** From the west on NY 28 in Arkville, turn south on Dry Brook Road (County Route 49) just west of Dry Brook Bridge, and travel 9.5 mi to the road's end. From the east on NY 28, turn south on County Route 49A at Belleayre Ski Center for about 5+ mi to County Route 49, turn left for 4.8 mi to road's end.

Parking and trailhead: Park at the snowplow turnabout. The trail register is just beyond the parking lot. ◀

Walk around a barrier gate. Dry Brook is very pretty here, with deep pools, unlike its name. This brook is never dry. The word comes from the German *drei brucke,* meaning "three bridges," which once spanned the brook. The yellow-marked trail follows the west side of the brook, reaching a miniature slide where trees could no longer cling to the steep hillside in a heavy storm and fell into the creek. A tributary from Drury Hollow is crossed on rocks.

The trail swings away from the stream through woods and then returns, reaching a lovely small waterfall and pool beyond Flatiron Brook. This tributary crossing over rocks could be difficult in high water. (A few yards upstream, a small tree over the water provides a handhold.) A little farther up the trail, a wooden bridge crosses Dry Brook at a spot where the rock formations and cascading water are quite a sight. Scamper down the bank before the bridge for a good view of the falls under it. The trail continues on the same (west) side of the brook on interesting flat rock. A small pothole was formed by swirling water and stone.

Here you can retrace, or if you want to try crossing Dry Brook for a longer walk to Shandaken lean-to, continue along a stony section of trail and fork right past road tracks. The trail soon crosses Dry Brook on rocks, possible in low water periods, but challenging. On the far side, do not follow the woods road, but head east up the slope to a second woods road above the north bank of Shandaken Brook, a tributary of Dry Brook. (Note the way, for your return trip.)

The grade is gradual to a fork, left, at 1.5 mi. Soon the trail descends to cross the brook, climbs and forks right. It enters state land at 2.0 mi, and crosses the brook again at 2.2 mi. Shandaken lean-to is located in an open, wooded, flat area above the water. Here you will retrace. (The trail climbs 600 more feet in 0.9 mi to the Pine Hill–West Branch Trail, connecting Balsam Mountain 4.0 mi north with other 3500-foot peaks with wooded summits.)

39. Lookouts on Dry Brook Ridge

Round-trip distance: 5.8 mi (9.4 km)
Elevation change: 1060 ft (323 m)
Summit elevation: 3400 ft (1037 m)
Difficulty: Moderate
Maps: Page 114; Trail Conference Map 42 (G-5); USGS Seager 7.5'

Summary: If you want solitude, try this off-the-beaten-track western section of the Catskills, where the mountains become hills and ridges. The trail offers nice views of a nearby reservoir as it meanders to the edge of Dry Brook Ridge.

▶ **Access to area:** From Arkville on NY 28, turn south on Dry Brook Road (County Route 49) immediately west of Dry Brook Bridge. Follow Dry Brook Road 6.1 mi to Mill Brook Road. Turn right and continue past the Dry Brook Ridge trailhead (at 2.2 mi) for about two more miles to Ploutz Road. (This is misidentified in the *New York State Atlas and Gazetteer.*) See last two paragraphs of this description for an alternate approach.

Parking and trailhead: Turn north on Ploutz Road for about two miles, past a home and barn and up a narrow dirt road to the trail register and parking area at right. The trail begins at the back of the parking area. (Do not descend across the road; the trail is marked in both directions.) ◀

Starting on the red-marked Huckleberry Loop Trail, head east upward through a pretty spruce and red pine forest. Emerging into an open deciduous woods, the trail climbs varying grades as it swings north toward Dry Brook Ridge, up a series of rocky ledges. Watch for red trail markers, which are plentiful. At times this new, little-used trail becomes obscure. The experience evokes what a woods ramble might have been like before trails were constructed. The grade eases

Waterfall beyond bridge, Dry Brook

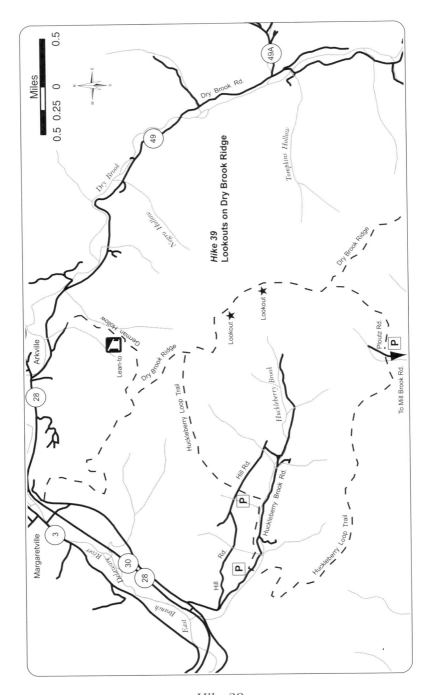

Hike 39

to gradual, a nice breather as you approach the junction at 1.4 mi, having ascended about 1000 ft. (We saw a horse here in mid-winter. He was found, in good condition, three days later.)

From the junction, turn left on the blue-marked Dry Brook Ridge Trail. You will be at one of the highest points on the ridge. The trail heads north for 0.9 mi on mostly level terrain to excellent views west over Cold Spring Hollow towards Pepacton Reservoir. Mill Brook Ridge is south and Mount Pisgah is to the right.

In an additional 0.4 mi, the trail swings over to the edge of an enormous drop. The best overlooks occur in the next 0.2 mi. Continue, descending occasionally, to a last, large ledge that affords plenty of room for sitting and enjoying lunch with a view. This is your turnaround point, 1.5 mi from the junction. (Beyond this spot the trail swings right into woods and descends.)

Another good approach to the Dry Brook Ridge lookouts is from Margaretville. It involves an additional 300-foot ascent and one extra mile, round-trip. Travel 2.2 mi west of Margaretville on NY 28/30 to a left turn. The road arrives promptly at a T intersection. Turn left again and proceed 0.3 mi to Huckleberry Brook Road. Turn right for another 0.3 mi, then at fork, bear left, up Hill Road for 1.3 mi, to a parking area across from a DEC sign.

The first 0.3 mi is a steady climb through a magnificent red pine forest, itself a worthy hike through stately trees on a soft pine-needle path. The ascent moderates through a variety of deciduous and evergreen stands until the trail turns right on an old woods road at 1.5 mi. Then it climbs steadily to 3100 ft, where you gain the ridge top at 1.9 mi. After another 0.4 mi of level terrain, turn right at the junction, heading south for 1.0 mi to a spectacular ledge, where you can sit and enjoy a well-earned rest and lunch. Retrace your steps from here.

40. Kelly Hollow

Round-trip distance: 4.0 mi (6.4 km)
Elevation change: 400 ft (122 m)
Difficulty: Moderately easy
Maps: Page 116; Trail Conference Map 42 (F-5); USGS Arena 7.5'

Summary: Kelly Hollow is off the beaten track, so this area doesn't get the attention it deserves. The entire hike is very attractive, with a variety of forest and terrain, beautiful streams, and a lean-to in a terrific setting.

Access to area: From Arkville on NY 28, turn south on Dry Brook Road immediately west of Dry Brook Bridge. Follow Dry Brook Road (County Route 49) 6.1 mi to Mill Brook Road. Turn right (continue past Dry Brook Ridge trailhead at 2.2 mi) for at least 5 mi to the first (east) access parking area at Kelly Hollow. From Old NY

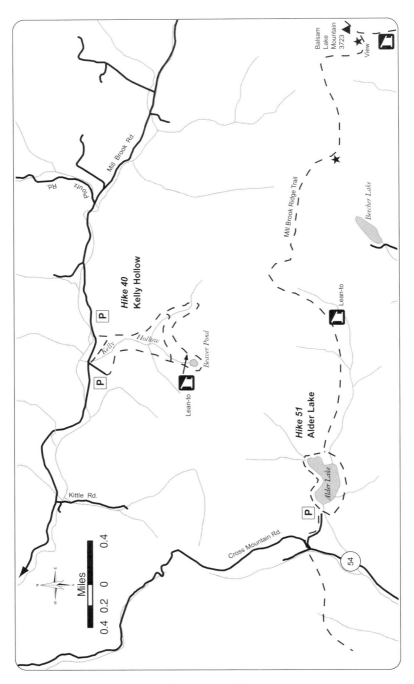

Hikes 40 and 51

30 (south side of Pepacton Reservoir), travel east 5.5 mi on Jim Alton Road and Mill Brook Road (past the first entrance).

Parking and trailhead: We suggest parking at the east access area because a trail register and privy are located here. Follow the yellow-marked trail into the conifer woods right of the privy.

In 0.2 mi through shady conifer woods, you reach the west access road into Kelly Hollow. Turn left on the access road. In the woods, left, are several attractive designated camping areas. Note a cemetery up on your right, and pass a barrier to climb the wide trail past stone walls through a hemlock forest. You come to a steep drop-off to the stream below. After a bridge crossing, the trail briefly steepens to the junction, 1.0 mi from your starting point.

Turn left here on the crossover trail, which is not to be missed, even if you plan to hike the long loop only. This short 0.2 mi crossover is beautiful, taking you along two streams through lovely forest. The trail drops steadily down the wide path to the first stream, crossing on a small bridge near delightful cascades. The level trail heads toward a second stream, which it crosses on a good bridge with a railing. As you ascend to the next junction, look left to the waterfall below.

At the junction turn right, hiking along level terrain with a wonderful contrast of woods: a dark spruce forest on the left and deciduous woods on the hillside above the stream. You come to a deep rock foundation, right, perhaps the old Kelly homestead. The trail swings right through tall conifers toward a hillside. After crossing a bridge, the trail loops back, gradually climbing the hill with views of the evergreen forest you've hiked through.

Through a hemlock woods the trail curves left on top of rock ledges. Trekking through the attractive forest, you reach the lean-to at 2.7 mi in a beautiful site with tall trees near Beaver Pond, complete with picnic table and fireplace. The pond was created by the stone dam, although past beaver activity is evident.

The yellow-marked trail continues left around the pond, crossing the small inlet brook originating on Mill Brook Ridge, above. (The new Mill Brook Ridge Trail traverses this ridge from Alder Lake to Balsam Lake Mountain.) Circling the pond, the trail descends a short 0.5 mi on gradual but steady grades back to the crossover junction. Turn right and cross again, so you descend via a different trail directly to your parking area.

Enjoy the streams; by now you may be ready to get wet. After crossing the bridge and ascending to the junction, turn left this time and descend on gradual grades past a yellow barrier gate. Turn left into the conifer forest, where camping is allowed. The trailhead is close by to the right.

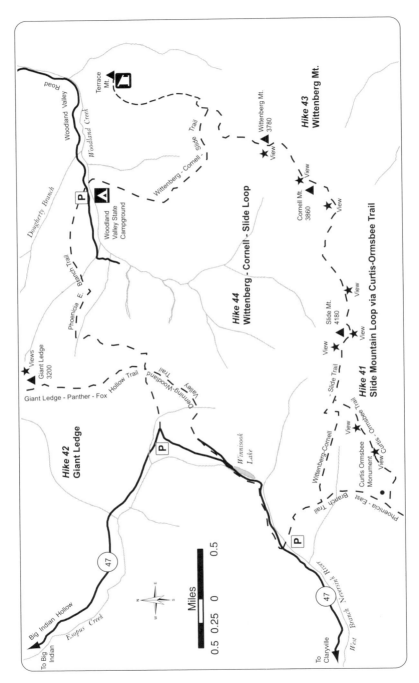

Hikes 41, 42, 43, and 44

"Nature we have always with us, an inexhaustible storehouse

of that which moves the heart, appeals to the mind,

and fires the imagination—health to the body,

a stimulus to the intellect, and a joy to the soul."

—JOHN BURROUGHS

South Catskills

The interior Catskills were initially overshadowed by the grand hotels built along the eastern rim of the Great Wall of Manitou in the 19th century. Yet this region offers many superlatives. Professor Guyot of Princeton University determined that Slide Mountain is the Catskill's highest peak at 4180 ft, kindling interest in this less developed area. The highest vertical ascent to a summit is 2623 ft to Peekamoose Mountain on the southern border of the Catskill Park. Trailheads are located along scenic, sparsely-populated county roads.

Naturalist John Burroughs' writings about the southern and western Catskills awakened national interest in this region. Woodsman, angler, guide, and writer, he so immersed himself in nature and conveyed that experience so effectively, that he gave his gift of observation as both a naturalist and a lover of the natural world to millions. Burroughs once said, "What we love to do, that we do well. To know is not all, it is only half. To love is the other half."

Born in 1837 near Roxbury, Burroughs met and married Ursula North and taught in the Hudson River Valley before accepting a position with the Treasury Department in Washington D.C. His prolific writing career began at age 28 with an essay on nature that was published by the *Atlantic Monthly*.

In the course of the next 56 years, Burroughs wrote three hundred essays, which filled twenty-seven books, while farming, traveling, and exploring the natural world. He expressed great concern about the course of the modern world, foreshadowing more contemporary sentiments: "One cannot but reflect what a sucked orange the earth will be in the course of a few more centuries. Our civilization is terribly expensive to all its natural resources; one hundred years of modern life exhausts its stores more than a millennium of the life of antiquity."

In 1899 Burroughs served as historian of the famed Harriman Expedition, a renowned group of writers, scientists, and artists who explored the Alaskan wilderness. An early member of the conservation movement in the United States,

Burroughs's friends and hiking companions included Walt Whitman, President Theodore Roosevelt, Thomas Edison, Andrew Carnegie, and Henry Ford. Today the United States Geological Survey officially recognizes the imposing three-peak mountain range of Slide, Cornell, and Wittenberg as the Burroughs Range.

If you have time after a hike, want a change of pace, or the weather isn't cooperating, consider one of the following attractions:

Karma Triyana Dharmachaka Monastery. At Lookout Mountain trailhead, Meads Mountain Road, Woodstock. Tours, 1:30 P.M., Sat. and Sun. 845-679-3400.

Woodstock Historical Society Museum. June 15–Oct. 15, 1–5 P.M. 845-679-2256.

Tubing the Esopus Creek. Transportation from Phoenicia upstream to tube the Esopus Creek past the village to the Catskill Mountain railroad, which brings you back to Phoenicia. Town Tinker, 845-688-5553, or F-S Tube Rental, 845-688-7633.

Catskill Mountain Railroad. A scenic, 6-mile round-trip rail ride along the Esopus Creek from Mountain Pleasant to Phoenicia. NY 28, Mt. Pleasant, NY.

Kenneth L. Wilson Campground. A public campground located off NY 28 near Boiceville. Swimming, nonmotorized boating.

Empire State Railway Museum. Phoenicia. Ulster and Delaware station with exhibits on the history of Catskill Mountain railroads. 845-688-7501.

Frost Valley YMCA. County Route 47, 13 mi south of Big Indian. Offers environmental education, including on-site research directed by the U.S. Geological Survey and the New York City Department of Environmental Protection. Summer camp, Family and Conference Center, year-round Elderhostel, and theme weekends. 845-985-2291, ext. 207. 2000 Frost Valley Rd., Claryville, NY 12725.

41. Slide Mountain Loop via Curtis-Ormsbee Trail

Round-trip distance: 6.7 mi (10.8 km)
Elevation change: 1780 ft (543 m)
Summit elevation: 4180 ft (1274 m)
Difficulty: Moderately strenuous
Maps: Page 118; Trail Conference Map 43 (J-6); USGS Shandaken 7.5'
    and Peekamoose Mountain 7.5'

Summary: Only two peaks in the Catskill Park have elevations higher than 4000 ft: Slide Mountain at 4180 ft and Hunter Mountain at 4040 ft. Yet the ascent to Slide is one of the easier climbs, because it starts at a higher elevation, and is only 2.8 mi. The upper reaches, adorned with evergreen on gradual slopes, offer splendid views of many of the mountains exceeding 3500 ft. It is spectacular up here on a sunny winter day. The Curtis-Ormsbee Trail offers good views, dramatic terrain, and a variety of forests.

▶ **Access to area:** From NY 28 at Big Indian, turn south on County Route 47 for 9.4 mi. From the south, on NY 55 2.0 mi west of Grahamsville, turn north on County Route 19 to Claryville. Turn left on County Route 157 over the East Branch of the Neversink (becomes County Route 47) for 11.5 mi.

Parking and trailhead: A large parking area is on the east side of County Route 47. Sign in at the trail register and follow the yellow-marked Phoenicia–East Branch Trail, also known as the Denning–Woodland Valley Trail. ◀

The yellow-marked Phoenicia–East Branch Trail crosses the West Branch of the Neversink River by rock-hopping. Sometimes this is challenging; at other times the riverbed is completely dry. The trail heads east on the level, then ascends rock slabs and ledges. The ascent is now much improved by new trail work. At 0.4 mi, stone steps climb to an old woods road. Turn right on this nearly level, rocky grade.

At 0.7 mi from the trailhead, turn left on the red-marked Wittenberg-Cornell-Slide Trail, hereafter referred to as the Slide Mountain Trail. Ascend gradually on rocky terrain through deciduous woods. At 1.2 mi, a sign indicates a campsite right. The grade steepens to the 3500-foot marker, and then it moderates and almost levels out briefly, for a nice breather. The trail ascends through balsam fir and swings north where it contours the slope, another welcome level section.

It curves east again, gradually ascending, and views open up to the north. The Curtis-Ormsbee Trail junction at 2.1 mi heads right, but *do not* turn here—keep going straight to the summit on grades varying from level to moderate. After gaining considerable ascent, note a rock ledge left of the trail 0.6 mi from the Curtis-Ormsbee junction. The ledge provides one of the finest views in the Catskills. From here, you can see nearby Giant Ledge and Panther, Sherrill, North Dome to the north, all of the Devils Path peaks, Black Dome, Blackhead, Kaaterskill High Peak to the northeast, Wittenberg, and Cornell to the east.

You are near the summit. After crossing a clearing that marks the true summit, the former site of a fire tower, you descend slightly to a great rock ledge. The profile of mountains on the northeast horizon, resembling a reclining figure, is called the Old Man of the Mountain. The densely wooded ridge of Friday Mountain, near to the east, connects over to Cornell. The Ashokan Reservoir spreads over the southern Catskills. Be sure to look at the John Burroughs Memorial Plaque at the base of this rock ledge. Among its observations is, "He made many visits to this peak and slept several nights beneath this rock." (For more on John Burroughs, see opening pages of this section and of Northwest Catskills.)

Descending 0.7 mi back to the blue-blazed Curtis-Ormsbee Trail junction, turn left. The trail heads southwest and slightly ascends before dropping down rocky pitches; then swings westerly for a pleasant walk along a long, gradually descending path through balsam woods. After traversing a meadow-like area with yellow birch, the trail drops down a steep pitch, 1.0 mi from the junction.

Look soon for a spur path left, marked by large flat rocks embedded in the trail, which leads to Pauls Lookout. These rock ledges provide fine views of Table Mountain and the ridge connecting it to Lone Mountain, one of the higher trail-less peaks. Rocky, Balsam Cap, and Friday Mountains are seen left of Lone Mountain over the Slide ridge. Immediately after this lookout is another sharp drop down rock ledges, so if you reach the second of two drops, retrace to find the view. Another perspective, west, from a rock ledge at 3450 ft, offers a good view of Doubletop in the distance. The trail drops precipitously through a maze of boulders. After more steady descent, the trail swings left to maneuver down a dramatic geological formation, rock walls you can walk between. Soon, you reach the junction of the yellow-marked Phoenicia–East Branch Trail. You've descended 900 ft in 1.6 mi from the junction to the monument to William Curtis and Allen Ormsbee, who cut this trail. They died in a snowstorm on Mount Washington in New Hampshire in June 1900.

Turn north (right) on the Phoenicia–East Branch Trail, which descends very gradually on rocky, wet footing. Conditions improve as the old road swings right downhill and crosses a bridge over a tributary of the West Branch of the Neversink. Continue straight on the yellow trail to the Slide Mountain Trail junction. From here, you're retracing the way you began. Turn left down the rock steps 0.3 mi farther, and retrace your steps 0.4 mi to the trailhead.

The Slide Mountain Trail is an ideal winter climb, with no steep ledges and a beautiful evergreen path near the summit. In addition, it is somewhat wind-protected at the summit. Some sections of the Curtis-Ormsbee Trail have steep ledges, and in winter you may prefer to retrace down the Slide Mountain Trail. Because Slide Mountain is an extremely popular climb, consider mid-week or off-season hiking for greater solitude.

42. Giant Ledge

Round-trip distance: first lookout, 3.0 mi (4.8 km); last overlook, 3.8 mi (6.1 km)
Elevation change: 1000 ft (305 m)
Summit elevation: 3200 ft (976 m)
Difficulty: Moderate
Maps: Page 118; Trail Conference Map 43 (J-6); USGS Shandaken 7.5'

Summary: Giant Ledge is one of the most satisfying short hikes in the Catskills. In only a mile and a half, you reach several lovely overlooks to nearby Cornell and Wittenberg Mountains, Woodland Valley, and sweeping views of the Hudson River Valley and northern mountains from large rock ledges which drop off hundreds of feet. You work a bit to gain this scenic area.

➤ **Access to area:** From NY 28, turn south on County Route 47 at Big Indian. Travel 7.4 mi to the hairpin turn. From the south, from NY 55 2.0 mi west of Grahamsville, turn north on County Route 19 to Claryville, turn left over the bridge on County Route 157 for 13.5 mi (becomes County Route 47). The trailhead is about 2.0 mi north of the Slide Mountain trailhead.

Parking and trailhead: Park in the DEC parking area located at the hairpin turn. Cross County Route 47 at the turn, and head east on the yellow-marked Phoenicia–East Branch Trail, also known as the Denning–Woodland Valley Trail. ◀

Beyond the trail register, the trail crosses a brook on a wide bridge. Take your time for the next 0.7 mi, for it is steady and sometimes steep climbing up 520 vertical feet. You gain ascent immediately, swinging northeast on rocky trail. A steep ascent up rock cobble, much improved by new trail work, brings you to the unmarked junction of the old Denning–Woodland Valley Trail..

Continue to the main junction at the DEC trail sign, and turn left on the blue-marked Giant Ledge–Panther–Fox Hollow Trail. The next 0.5 mi is a welcome breather through attractive woods on level trail. The trail ascends on moderate and steep grades through picturesque rock outcrops to the area of Giant Ledge. This high plateau features eight excellent lookouts in the next 0.4 mi southeast to Wittenberg and Cornell peaks and expansive views overlooking the Hudson River Valley—with Overlook, Indian Head, Twin, Sugarloaf, and Plateau Mountains from east to west. Slide Mountain can be seen to the south from some of the overlooks. Explore the area; camping is allowed on this broad, flat area.

(The ambitious can continue 1.5 mi to Panther Mountain, losing ascent to a col and reclimbing 725 ft. There is a fine lookout 100 ft right of the trail about halfway to Panther, and the same magnificent vista east and north, but no view west, from the 3720-foot summit.)

43. Wittenberg Mountain

Round-trip distance: 7.8 mi (12.6 km)
Elevation change: 2430 ft (741 m)
Summit elevation: 3780 ft (1153 m)
Difficulty: Difficult, with two steep ascents up cliffs
Maps: Page 118; Trail Conference Map 43 (K-6); USGS Phoenicia 7.5'

Summary: This climb offers magnificent 180-degree views and spectacular terrain. The climb to Wittenberg Mountain is an exciting challenge. Two areas in the upper third of the climb involve extremely steep scrambles up rock ledges. After 3.9 mi to the summit, you feel you've earned this one. You will need good boots and plenty of water.

Icy conditions prevail on this north approach to Wittenberg until well into spring. Winter climbs on these very steep ledges require full crampons and packable snow texture to create stable footing.

▶ **Access to area:** Turn south off NY 28 just west of Phoenicia at the Woodland Valley Public Campground sign. Cross the Esopus Creek bridge and turn right on Woodland Valley Road for 4.7 mi.

Parking and trailhead: A large parking lot is on the right before the entrance to the campground. A day-use parking fee is charged (although it is waived if you are camping here). The trailhead is left, across the road, following a macadam service road. Follow red DEC trail markers, turning left on a gravel path right of campsite 45 to the bridge across Woodland Creek. ◀

Climbing begins as soon as you cross the bridge over Woodland Creek. Sign the trail register at 0.2 mi. The climb continues quite steeply after the register. At 0.5 mi, the grade eases as you enter an area of interesting rock outcrops and shady hemlock woods, with views east to Terrace Mountain.

At 1.0 mi, note that the trail turns left, going up a rocky hillside, instead of following a wide trail straight ahead. Swinging nearly south, the trail climbs away from the cliffs, ascends gradual grades for another mile and then levels for the last 0.5 mi to the Terrace Mountain junction at 2.6 mi. Turn right here, climbing gradually around the hillside and then swinging south to begin the adventure of the final third of your hike to the summit!

This is a section of several increasingly vertical scrambles up rock cliffs. At the top of the second pitch upward, follow the re-routed trail left which leads to good views north to Sherrill, North Dome, Black Dome, Blackhead, and the Devils Path peaks. Soon, the trail ascends two cliff-like areas, first up a sharp rock cut and then maneuvering up a very steep rock bluff. Take care in these places, and look to the right for the trail if you reach a rock wall.

After these challenges, the trail settles down to being merely steep, but very scenic, as it maneuvers up myriad mossy ledges. Finally leveling through a very pretty area, you break out of the woods onto a large open area of flat rock, which is one of the magnificent 180-degree views in the Catskills. From the north rock, you can see the Blackhead Range in the distance (Thomas Cole, Black Dome, and Blackhead), Hunter, Plateau, Sugarloaf, Twin, Indian Head, Plattekill, Overlook, and Kaaterskill High Peak behind Sugarloaf. The Ashokan Reservoir spreads out to the southeast beyond Samuels Point, a smaller peak. Looking south to southwest, you can see Friday, Balsam Cap, Peekamoose, and Table Mountains.

44. Wittenberg–Cornell–Slide Loop from Woodland Valley

Round-trip distance: 15.0 mi (24.2 km)
Elevation change: 4020 ft (1226 m)
Summit elevations: Wittenberg, 3780 ft (1153 m); Cornell, 3860 ft (1177 m);
    Slide, 4180 ft (1274 m)
Difficulty: Extremely difficult
Maps: Page 118; Trail Conference Map 43 (K-6); USGS Phoenicia 7.5', Peekamoose
Mountain 7.5', and Shandaken 7.5'

Summary: The most strenuous hike in this book. A three-mountain traverse on a 15-mile loop that returns to its original trailhead. This trek involves four or five challenging scrambles, ranging from 15 to 35 feet, up cliff-like ledges and rock outcrops. The hiker needs excellent boots, plenty of water, and stamina.

▶ **Access to area:** Turn south off NY 28 just west of Phoenicia at the Woodland Valley Public Campground sign. Cross the Esopus Creek bridge and turn right on Woodland Valley Road for 4.7 mi.

Parking and trailhead: A large parking lot is on the right before the entrance to the campground. A day-use parking fee is charged (although it is waived if you are camping here). The trailhead is left across the road, following a macadam service road. Follow red DEC markers, turning left on a gravel path right of campsite 45 to the bridge across Woodland Creek. ◀

See the ascent to Wittenberg (Hike 43) for the first 3.9 mi. Leaving the spectacular summit of Wittenberg, the trail heads west from the lookout, descending easily to a col between Cornell and Wittenberg. A first scramble up ledges is soon followed by a deep V-cut in a cliff nearly 15 ft high. Your boot must be wedged in the cut halfway up, while long, strong arms must reach the top to pull up—the cut lacks handholds.

Soon, a blue-marked spur path, 0.8 mi from Wittenberg, turns left to a partial view northeast at the 3860-foot summit of Cornell. Better views await just 0.1 mi down the trail. A 180-degree view towards Slide Mountain rewards the hiker, with Peekamoose and Table Mountains to the southwest, and Panther, Sherrill, North Dome, West Kill, Hunter, and the Blackhead Range to the north. A good second lookout is just below, followed by a narrow "lemon-squeezer."

In about 1.5 mi and a 610-foot descent, passing several trails to designated campsites, you reach the col. Other sites are located in attractive grassy and flat rock locations as you ascend Slide. About 0.4 mi from the col, you reach a 35-foot vertical rock outcrop that is difficult to ascend. You can wedge a boot on one rock step in a narrow crevice. The next step is too high for some, but you can kneel on the ledge and then stand to reach areas near or at the top. Another

15-foot vertical bluff also requires care.

Gradual and moderate grades lead to increasingly excellent views and a wonderful ice-cold spring which pours out of the rock wall at the end of a 25-foot blue-marked spur trail. (Only rarely is this much-appreciated source dry, although we have seen it so.) Four well-constructed ladders assist the hiker to the next level, a ledge from which Cornell and Wittenberg look spectacular near to the east over a deep valley.

A few more scrambles for 0.2 mi lead to the base of the lookout rock shelf at 7.0 mi. See Hike 41 for descriptions of the summit views and the red-marked Slide Mountain Trail which descends easily, on increasingly rocky footing, to the yellow-marked Phoenicia–East Branch Trail, where you turn right for 0.3 mi and then left down stone steps and recent trail work to the Slide Mountain trailhead.

You follow the Phoenicia–East Branch Trail onto County Route 47, heading right (northeast) for 1.0 mi uphill to the Winnisook Club. Continue just past the fenced lake area, and cross the road to a woods road with a sign showing an easement for public use. Follow this woods road, the old Denning–Woodland Valley Trail, for more than 1.5 mi to a junction, right, with DEC signs. You will continue east and north on the yellow-marked Phoenicia–East Branch Trail, which soon begins its steady descent back to the Woodland Valley parking area in 2.7 mi.

45. Peekamoose Trail to Overlook Ledge

Round-trip distance: 6.0 mi (9.7 km)
Elevation change: 2330 ft (710 m)
High-point elevation: 3530 ft (1076 m)
Difficulty: Moderately strenuous
Maps: Page 127; Trail Conference Map 43 (J-8);
    USGS Peekamoose Mountain 7.5′

Summary: Drive through scenic back roads to a stiff climb up to a magnificent view. The trek seems easier than its 2300-foot ascent indicates.

▶ **Access to area:** From NY 28, turn west on NY 28A at Boiceville and travel to West Shokan. Turn west on County Route 42 and follow it west for 10.1 mi, where it becomes a scenic, slower-paced road.

Parking and trailhead: DEC parking area is on the north side of the road. ◀

A steady ascent on the blue-marked Peekamoose-Table Trail begins immediately up an old woods road to the trail register. The trail continues at this grade through an open deciduous woods for 0.4 mi. These lower slopes were pasture until the 1920s; remains of an old foundation are seen, left. Soon, the trail

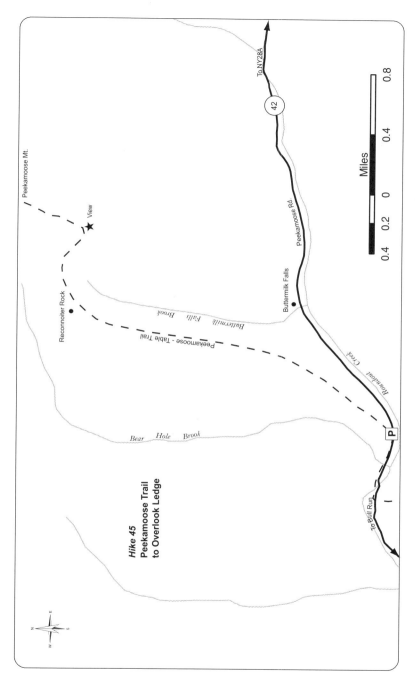

Hike 45
Peekamoose Trail
to Overlook Ledge

Peekamoose Mt.

View

Reconnoiter Rock

Bear Hole Brook

Peekamoose - Table Trail

Brook

Buttermilk Falls

Buttermilk Falls

Peekamoose Rd.

Rondout Creek

P

To Bull Run

42

To NY28A

Miles

0.4   0.2   0   0.4   0.8

N
W   E
S

Hike 45

becomes nearly level. Where the old road forks left, the trail becomes a path through a stand of tall red pines.

Passing a huge flat slab and interesting sedimentary formation with horizontal and diagonal layering, you gradually ascend a south ridge of Peekamoose. Terrain drops away to valleys not far from the trail on both sides. Short, steep pitches up through cliff-like ledges alternate with gradual plateaus where you get welcome breathers.

At Reconnoiter Rock 1.9 mi up, a balanced rock teeters on the edge of big ledges, tempting some to climb it. Views here are only through trees, but the broad flat rocks invite a break for snacks and cooling off. The terrain above Reconnoiter Rock changes character, turning east along a flat stretch through berry bushes, fern, and hobblebush. A spur path right leads to an overlook, best when leaves are off the trees. The trail reaches a jumble of conglomerate rock where partial views north toward Van Wyck and Table Mountains can be seen through the trees.

From here, the trail climbs steadily for 0.4 mi to the 3500-foot elevation marker. A short scramble up leads to the wide ledge, your destination, with excellent views northwest to Doubletop, Balsam Lake, and Van Wyck Mountains. You have climbed 2330 ft, higher than many Catskill summit ascents. The 2623-foot ascent to Peekamoose's summit, 3843 ft, is the greatest in the Catskills. Take time to explore this large plateau. The original steep trail to Peekamoose, now overgrown, is just a bit farther along the trail, coming up from the right. The current trail was cut by Pete Fish, a long-time forest ranger in the Catskills and in the Adirondacks' high peaks area.

If you wish to continue one more mile to the summit, it is 300 ft higher over level, then steep, terrain through attractive woods. The summit is covered with conifers. Spur paths, right, lead to views before the summit. Peekamoose is a very nice winter ascent, after a good blanketing of snowfall softens the ledges and allows sliding descents in the open woods.

Retrace to your car. Be sure to visit the beautiful pool across the road, a small distance to the left, a great spot to cool off after a long hike on a hot day. Note Buttermilk Falls a bit farther east. The waterfall has a subterranean source; water pours out of an opening in the cliff.

46. Ashokan High Point

Round-trip distance: 7.4 mi (11.9 km); with extension to cobble, 8.4 mi (13.5 km)
Elevation change: 2070 ft (631 m); with extension to cobble, 2520 ft (768 m)
Summit elevation: 3080 ft (939 m)
Difficulty: Strenuous
Maps: Page 130; Trail Conference Map 43 (K-8); USGS West Shokan 7.5'

Summary: In the 1800s there were plans to build a hotel on Ashokan High Point. Climb here when leaves are off the trees in higher altitudes, and you will appreciate why a hotel was considered for this site. This isolated peak at the southern border of the Catskill Park is a stiff climb in places, but in fall, winter, and spring, excellent views abound from several areas. Hike the extension to the open rock cobble in summer for best viewing.

▶ **Access to area:** From NY 28, take NY 28A at Boiceville west to its junction with County Route 42 in West Shokan. Follow County Route 42 for 3.9 mi.

Parking and trailhead: A large DEC parking lot is on the north side of the road. Cross the road and the bridge over Kanape Brook to the trail register. ◀

From the barrier gate, the red-marked trail, an old road, drops down to Kanape Brook and crosses over a bridge. The woods road follows the north bank of the brook on the level, then gradually ascends above the brook with occasional steady climbing. Several small tributaries drop to Kanape Brook. Mountain laurel abounds along this trail. Old stonework gives evidence of by-gone settlements.

After crossing a culvert, you enter a shady hemlock forest on level terrain, a good breather. The trail passes near Kanape Brook for a short distance. Reaching deciduous woods, you can see glimpses of your destination, left. The trail swings left and gradually climbs east to beautiful level woods filled with mountain laurel at 2.7 mi.

Watch here for a sharp turn left, but you continue straight. Steep climbing now begins, and again the trail turns left. After a very steep scramble up ledges, the trail alternates between nearly level areas and short steep pitches, amidst blueberry bushes and increasing mountain laurel. The summit often seems imminent but remains elusive, with the trail finally topping out at 3.7 mi.

Trees partially obstruct views, so ascend Ashokan High Point when leaves are off the trees in higher reaches (the summit trees are deciduous.) Hike the trail in winter if you have sufficient experience and winter equipment, including crampons for climbing up and down steep icy pitches. The views are magnificent, especially if you follow the red-marked trail north to an open field where the vista of Ashokan Reservoir and of many peaks north and east on a clear winter day is spectacular.

We recommend a side trip from Ashokan's summit to East Ashokan Lookout,

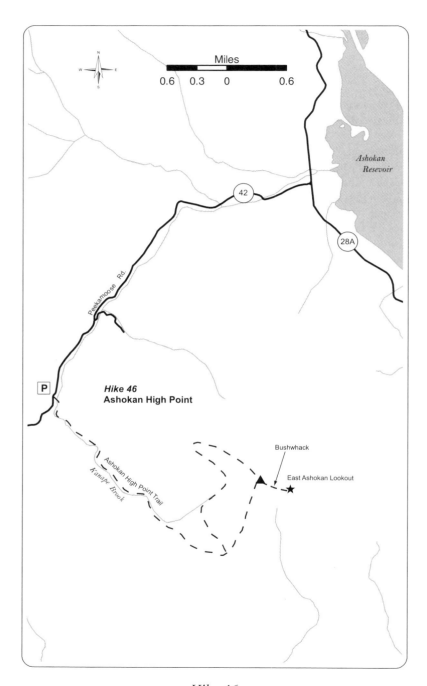

Hike 46

a 25-minute bushwhack down 325 ft at 120 degrees magnetic, then up a very short pitch to an open rock cobble with expansive views east, south, and west. In winter, views of the Ashokan Reservoir and as far north as the Devil's Path are magnificent. To get there, find a path heading east and descending from the summit ledge, to left of the view. The path is briefly obscured a little way down, but bear right and stay along the top of the ridge and you will find good paths taking you to this wonderful open area. You will want to spend time here, so allow an hour or two for this side trip. This area should be called Blueberry Cobble.

Retrace to the summit from the cobble, then descend the way you came.

47. Biscuit Brook Bushwhack

Round-trip distance: About 2.0 mi (3.2 km)
Elevation change: 675 ft (206 m) over ridge and back
Difficulty: Moderate
Maps: Page 132; Trail Conference Map 43 (I-7); USGS Peekamoose Mountain 7.5'

Summary: A mini-gorge created by the narrow rock walls of Biscuit Brook, with cascades falling into a deep clear pool. Starting on a marked trail, this off-trail option is so beautiful that we include it for those who love deep, cold swimming holes in mountain brooks. Bring a compass and wear boots with ankle protection.

▶ **Access to area:** From NY 28 at Big Indian, turn south on County Route 47 for 12.8 mi to the Pine Hill–West Branch Trail parking area on the southeast side of the road. From Claryville, travel north on County Route 157/47 for 8.1 mi to the parking area. Consult DeLorme's *New York State Atlas and Gazetteer* for possible approaches from the south.

Parking and trailhead: From the large DEC parking area, cross the road and walk northeast 100 ft to the trailhead. ◀

This route follows the blue-marked Pine Hill–West Branch Trail (also known as the Biscuit Brook–Pine Hill Trail) 0.8 mi to the top of a ridge, ascending 375 vertical feet, then leaves the trail and heads down to Biscuit Brook.

Leaving the road, the marked trail gradually ascends over rocky ground and crosses several small brooks in the first 0.5 mi, and then climbs more steeply to the ridgetop. At a sharp right turn in the trail, there is an arrow. Here, another unmarked trail heads southwest. Do not follow either trail, but bushwhack straight down the other side of the ridge for about 0.3 mi. Near to your left, on trees, you may see the property markings of the Frost Valley YMCA; stay to the right, in the Forest Preserve. Tangled undergrowth and rocky ground make for

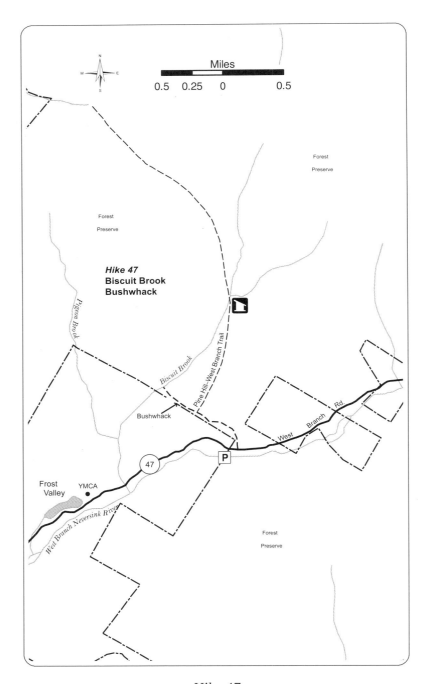

Hike 47

unstable footing, so take your time.

After descending steadily for 300 vertical feet, you reach picturesque Biscuit Brook. Look for broad rocky ledges along the brookside. **Exercise caution**; the rock is very slippery when wet. Beyond a narrowing of the watercourse, the way down to the pool is not notably slippery, although test your footing. The pool is very deep and you can swim up into the tiny gorge in the clear green water. This is a magical spot we discovered while bushwhacking to the trailless peak, Doubletop.

Return via your route of descent, avoiding the private property, indicated by tree blazes, on your right. Find the blue-marked DEC trail heading east-southeast (not north) back to the trailhead.

48. Red Hill

Round-trip distance: 2.8 mi (4.5 km)
Elevation change: 890 ft (271 m)
Summit elevation: 2990 ft (912 m)
Difficulty: Moderately easy
Maps: Page 134; Trail Conference Map 43 (H-8); USGS Claryville 7.5′

Summary: This relatively new trail, established by the DEC with the help of the New York–New Jersey Trail Conference, offers a delightful moderate hike up a small mountain in the southeastern Catskill Forest Preserve. Its destination is one of the five renovated Catskill fire towers.

▶ **Access to area:** From NY 55 west of Grahamsville, travel north on County Route 19 to Claryville and right on Red Hill Road to Coons Road. From NY 28 in Big Indian, travel south on County Route 47 for 20.9 mi to Claryville, becoming County Route 157. Turn left on County Route 19. Turn right up Red Hill Road for approximately 3.0 mi to Coons Road.

Parking and trailhead: Turn left up Coons Road for 1.2 mi, over a height of land, and continue 1.0 mi down the steep, narrow dirt road to the parking area on the left. Note: This last mile could pose a significant challenge in wet or icy conditions. ◀

A self-guiding nature trail is now featured here, and an informational brochure is available at the trailhead.

Follow yellow markers generally west over initially rocky ground. Soon the trail climbs up through ledges on varying grades to a level section. When the trail swings south, you gain ascent moderately to a very gradual trek around the hillside. Views begin to open through trees.

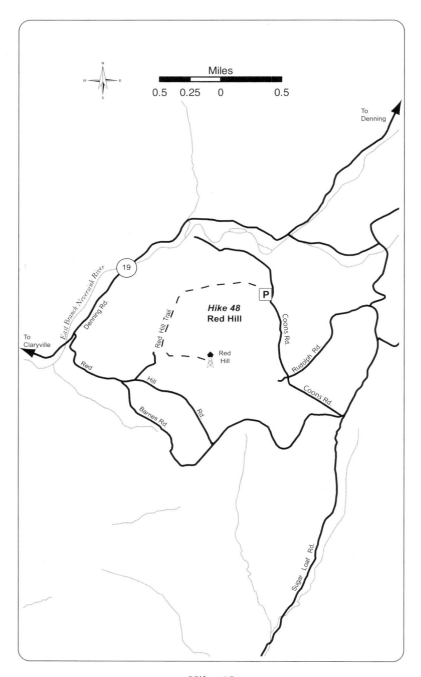

Hike 48

Steeper climbing brings you to the cabin and picnic table. The renovated 60-foot fire tower in the clearing beyond provides wonderful views to the Burroughs Range to the northeast, Peekamoose and Table to the east, Doubletop, Graham, and Balsam Lake Mountains to the northwest. To the south, expansive views feature sections of the Rondout Reservoir, the Shawangunk ridge and, with binoculars, Mohonk's Sky Top Tower.

DEC Forest Ranger Pete Fish served the Red Hill area before transfer to the Adirondack High Peaks region. The restored observer's cabin has many interesting pictures and stories about Red Hill's past. Red Hill's fire lookout station functioned from 1920 to 1990 and it was the last staffed tower in the Catskill Forest Preserve.

The tower has been renovated, is maintained by volunteers, and is sometimes staffed by volunteer observers. For more information, call 845-985-7274 or write the Red Hill Fire Tower Committee, c/o Helen and George Elias, P.O. Box 24, Grahamsville, NY 12740.

49. Vernooy Kill Falls

Round-trip distance: 3.6 mi (5.8 km)
Elevation change: 600 ft (183 m)
Difficulty: Moderately easy
Maps: Page 137; USGS Kerhonkson 7.5'

Summary: This hike is part of the Long Path, which starts near New York City and is being extended all the way to established trails in the Adirondacks. This section is the southernmost portion within the Catskill Park. It is a lovely hike through verdant mountain laurel to a beautiful series of cascades, with camping areas, an old stonework mill, and many old-growth white pines. Pick a very hot day and enjoy a swim in natural mountain pools.

▶ **Access to area:** From NY 209, travel north on County Route 3 (Pataukunk Road, also known as Samsonville Road). Beyond the hamlet of Mombaccus, turn left at an intersection 3.4 mi from NY 209. In 0.2 mi, bear left at the fork with Ridgeview Road. Drive another 0.6 mi, passing two more side roads. Stay left at each junction. After a small bridge, turn right at a three-way junction onto Upper Cherrytown Road and continue north another 3.1 mi, a total of 7.8 mi from NY 209. If approaching from the north (NY 28A), use DeLorme's *New York State Atlas and Gazetteer* and the following paragraph, but note that these back roads are especially poorly marked. See last two paragraphs of this hike description for an alternate hiking approach to the waterfall itself.

From NY 28A south of Ashokan Reservoir, take County Route 3 south to Upper

Cherrytown Road south of Samsonville. Turn right and follow this winding road to the trailhead parking area south of Riggsville.

Parking and trailhead: The parking area is on the south side of Upper Cherrytown Road. Cross road to trailhead and follow red trail markers into the woods. ◀

The trail slightly descends 0.2 mi to a brook. Rock hop across and continue along the old road. (The stream, right, is not the Vernooy Kill.) The road can be wet. If necessary, a side path left connects to the road as it curves left up the hillside. Swinging right, the ascent continues, surrounded by mountain laurel, to a welcome level section.

Then another steady ascent climbs to a shady hemlock woods, again with brief wet trail from hillside runoff. The path winds through a grove of small beech, ascending on a gradual grade to the ridgetop. Swinging left around the end of the ridge, the now-level walk becomes delightful, surrounded by a profusion of mountain laurel. Note the huge white pines by the trail. Soon, sounds of the Vernooy Kill can be heard. On the left are designated campsites in a lovely setting of large white pine, with fire pits, log benches, and stone shelves for cooking.

Crossing a small stream on rocks, you arrive at this beauty spot, with gorgeous cascading falls rushing through overhanging ledges. An old stone mill evokes memories of a bygone era. A path along the brook before the bridge takes you to upper cascades with pools to swim in. Across the sturdy bridge, you can explore up and down the stream. Note the huge white pine across from the mill, with gigantic roots spreading over a rock ledge.

(The main trail heads right before the bridge. A substantial stone foundation is up in the woods left off the main trail.)

Another nice approach to Vernooy Kill Falls is along a snowmobile trail from Greenville. From NY 55 at Rondout Reservoir, take NY 55A to County Route 53. In Sundown, travel about 5 mi east on County Route 46. (If accessing NY 55A at the east end of the reservoir, travel to County Route 46 and turn north to Greenville.)

Where County Route 46 turns 90 degrees (west or south), turn into Dymond Road and park on the left. The trail is across the road, and heads east. You descend gradually on a wide old road through an attractive forest for 2.0 mi to the bridge over Vernooy Falls.

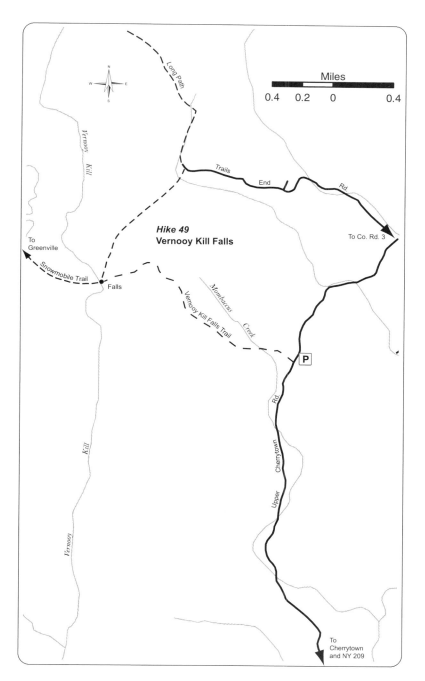

Miles

0.4   0.2   0   0.4

Long Path

Vernooy Kill

Trails End Rd.

To Co. Rd. 3

**Hike 49
Vernooy Kill Falls**

To
Greenville

Snowmobile Trail

Falls

Vernooy Kill Falls Trail

Montbaccus Creek

P

Kill

Upper Cherrytown Rd.

Vernooy Kill

To
Cherrytown
and NY 209

Hike 49

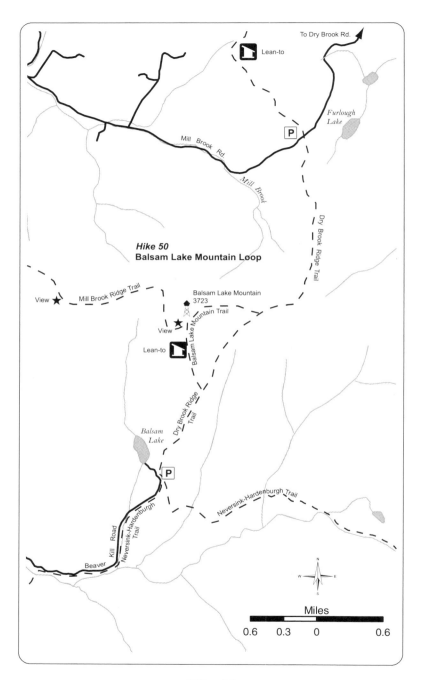

To Dry Brook Rd.

Lean-to

Furlough
Lake

Mill Brook Rd

P

Mill Brook

Dry Brook Ridge Trail

Hike 50
Balsam Lake Mountain Loop

View ★ Mill Brook Ridge Trail

Balsam Lake Mountain
3723

View ★ Balsam Lake Mountain Trail

Lean-to

Balsam
Lake

Dry Brook Ridge Trail

P

Neversink-Hardenburgh Trail

Neversink-Hardenburgh Trail

Kill Road

Neversink-Hardenburgh Trail

Beaver

N
W   E
S

Miles

0.6   0.3   0   0.6

Hike 50

"Nature furnishes the conditions—the solitude

—and the soul furnishes the entertainment."

—JOHN BURROUGHS

Southwest Catskills

Miles of trails in this region offer good hiking and cross-country skiing opportunities. Trails can be combined for loops ranging from leisurely (Frick Pond) to all-day excursions (Quick Lake). Three public campgrounds are near world-renowned fly-fishing streams. Two fish hatcheries are open to the public. Many ponds and lakes have trails around their periphery, and nonmotorized boating is allowed. Several covered bridges, built in the 1860s, still span trout streams.

If you have time after a hike, want a change of pace, or the weather isn't cooperating, consider one of the following attractions:

Little Pond Public Campground. Swimming, nonmotorized boating, fishing. From Livingston Manor on NY 17, travel 14.0 mi north on County Routes 151, 152, and 54 (the route number changes in each county), turning north on Barkaboom Road. From NY 28 or NY 30, take Old NY 30, south of Pepacton Reservoir, to Barkaboom Road. Turn left for several miles.

Mongaup Pond Public Campground. Swimming, nonmotorized boating, fishing. From Route 17 (Quickway), take exit 96 at Livingston Manor, turn left on County Route 81/82 and proceed to DeBruce. Turn north on Mongaup Road after nearly 4.0 mi.

Beaverkill Public Campground. Swimming, picnicking, and fishing access. Beaverkill Road, near Lew Beach.

Beaverkill Covered Bridge. A 118-foot span over the Beaverkill River. Of lattice-type construction, it was built in 1865. Part of Beaverkill Public Campground, on Beaverkill Road near Lew Beach.

Alder Lake. Camping, nonmotorized boating, hiking. Alder Lake Road (County Route 54) 2.6 mi north of Beaverkill Road from Turnwood.

Beaverkill Trout Hatchery. Alder Lake Road, 0.2 mi north of Beaverkill Road from Turnwood. Raises five varieties of trout: rainbow, golden rainbow, brook, brown, and tiger. Viewing open to the public.

Catskill State Fish Hatchery. One of twelve fish hatcheries in New York State, run by the Department of Environmental Conservation. The Catskill hatchery specializes in raising brown trout, producing 1,350,000 fish annually. Fish Hatchery Road, Debruce, off County Route 81 east of Livingston Manor. Open to public year round, 8:30 A.M.–4 P.M. weekdays and 8:30 A.M.–noon on summer weekends and holidays. 845-439-4328.

Catskill Fly Fishing Center and Museum. NY 17 Exit 96W or Exit 94 east to Old NY 17, between Livingston Manor and Roscoe. Exhibits, catch and release area, children's education weekends. 845-439-4810.

Roscoe O. and W. Railway Museum. Exhibits, theater shows. Roscoe, NY 17. 607-498-5500.

Livingston Manor Covered Bridge Park. A 103-ft span over the Willowemoc Creek, built in 1860 and restored in 1985. Park offers fishing access, picnicking, and pavilion. NY 17, Livingston Manor. Exit 96, turn right for 0.4 mi and right on Old NY 17 for 1.0 mi. Turn left.

50. Balsam Lake Mountain Loop

Round-trip distance: 4.3 mi (6.9 km)
Elevation change: 1190 ft (363 m)
Summit elevation: 3720 ft (1134 m)
Difficulty: Moderate
Maps: Page 138; Trail Conference Map 43 (G-6); USGS Seager 7.5'

Summary: A loop over the westernmost of the Catskill high peaks, those over 3500 ft, to a renovated fire tower offering views of the southern Catskills. Fine views east to several high peaks open up on the descent, and Dry Brook Ridge Trail offers views down the steep mountainside to Black Brook Valley.

▶ **Access to area:** From NY 17 (Quickway), exit 96 at Livingston Manor, take the first two right turns. Proceed 0.3 mi, then turn right just past Kings Catering. Continue for 14.0 mi on County Routes 151, 152, and 54 (same road) to a junction with Barkaboom Road and Beaver Kill Road. Turn east on Beaver Kill Road and proceed approximately 9 mi to the end of the road. From NY 28/30 in Margaretville, travel west to old NY 30 (where NY 28/30 curves right), turn left, traveling *south* of Pepacton Reservoir to Barkaboom Road. Turn left and continue for several miles past Little Pond Public Campground to Beaver Kill Road. Turn left for approximately 9 mi to the end of the road. Enjoy the drive along Beaver Kill Road, as it winds next to a beautiful trout stream, with cascading falls and pools. Look for deer and blue heron.

Parking and trailhead: The road dead-ends at the DEC parking area. The trail heads north. Avoid the road to the Balsam Lake Angler's Club. ◀

The trail starts out easily alongside a fern-filled meadow, then begins ascending through open woods to a junction at 0.9 mi, gaining 400 ft. This is the halfway point to the summit. Turn left on the red-marked trail and begin steeper climbing through blackberry bushes and ferns. At 1.3 mi, a spur trail left leads to the Balsam Lake Mountain lean-to and privy. A spring bursts out a short distance up the main trail (except in dry seasons). A bit more climbing leads to a spur trail, right, to the site of former lean-tos.

Continuing north on the red-marked trail, the route becomes a delightful, very gradual ascent through a fragrant spruce and balsam grove. At 1.7 mi, you reach the junction with the Mill Brook Ridge Trail from Alder Lake, completed in spring 1998. A fine view west can be found 0.1 mi on this yellow-marked trail, which is part of the Finger Lakes Trail. Retracing to the red-marked trail, you are close to the summit, covered with spruce and mountain ash.

The renovated fire tower, dedicated in June 2000, now affords great views north to many 3500-foot peaks, and nearby to Graham and Doubletop, two of the highest trailless peaks. After your break, continue your loop, heading east off the summit. In 0.3 mi, a good view opens up to Graham, Doubletop, and Big Indian Mountains. From here, the descent is steady for 0.5 mi to a junction with blue-marked Dry Brook Ridge Trail.

Turn right on the blue trail, descending on gradual grades, at first on rocky footing. The mountainside drops ever more steeply down to Black Brook Valley. Vistas open up across the drop to the south and east. The trail becomes a gentle, grassy path back to the first junction. Here, continue straight for 0.9 mi back to your car.

The mountain can also be ascended from the north, climbing south up Dry Brook Ridge Trail. To reach the Dry Brook Ridge trailhead, head south from NY 28 in Arkville on Dry Brook Road (County Route 49), just west of the Dry Brook bridge, and continue for 6.1 mi. Turn right on Mill Brook Road for 2.2 mi to the DEC parking area at right. Cross the road to the blue-marked trail.

This makes an excellent ski or snowshoe route on a wide lane up gradual and moderate grades, but it is wise to avoid this trail in hunting season. A spring is located a bit downhill and to the right in 1.2 mi, then a mile-long level section brings you to the red-marked Balsam Lake Mountain Trail junction, which climbs right for 0.8 mi to the summit. (Dry Brook Ridge Trail descends to the south trailhead of Balsam Lake Mountain; see loop hike above.)

51. Alder Lake

Round-trip distance: 1.5 mi (2.4 km)
Elevation change: Slight ascent around south side of lake
Difficulty: Easy
Maps: Page 116; Trail Conference Map 42 (F-6); USGS Arena 7.5'

Summary: The large, abandoned Coykendall Lodge still remains near the lake-front. A shoreline path heads north along the attractive lake, with occasional well-spaced campsites allowing for a degree of privacy all around the lake. This is a fine place to fish or canoe, have a picnic, and explore the lakefront, with lots of frogs and salamanders.

▶ **Access to area:** From NY 17 (Quickway), exit 96 at Livingston Manor, take first two right turns. Proceed 0.3 mi and make right turn just past Kings Catering. Continue 14.3 mi (past Barkaboom Road). Turn north onto County Route 54 at the junction at Turnwood. (You might want to stop at the fish hatchery. They have five types of trout: rainbow, golden rainbow, tiger, brook, and brown.) Continue 2.4 mi and bear right at curve at Cross Mountain Camp; at immediate second junction, do not go up hill but bear right for 0.4 mi.

Parking and trailhead: Gravel road terminates at Alder Lake Trailhead parking area, left. A trail register is at the beginning of a short road that leads to impressive remains of the old lodge on Alder Lake. ◀

Follow a path to the shore, dam, and DEC sign. Turn north away from the dam and proceed along the shoreline path. You soon arrive at the first of several designated campsites. Follow red trail markers along the lake. After crossing a few bridges on the far side, bear left at a narrow fork and then right onto a broad woods road. The trail ascends gradually (bearing right at forks), passing old stone walls from a bygone era. At 0.7 mi, the Mill Brook Ridge Trail leaves for Balsam Lake Mountain, 5.8 mi away.

Descending to a bridge over Alder Lake's inlet, you soon pass a campsite 250 ft toward the lake. The trail gradually ascends for 0.2 mi, about 250 ft from the shore. After crossing another small bridge at 1.2 mi, there is another campsite. Then the trail swings right to return to your starting point, crossing the outlet dam. Two other campsites can be found by turning right before the railing, crossing the field, and following a path into the woods.

This is an excellent trail for skiing or snowshoeing, with several other woods roads nearby to explore on skis.

52. Little Pond to Touchmenot Mountain View

Round-trip distance: 3.0 mi (4.8 km)
Elevation change: 350 ft (107 m)
High-point elevation: 2350 ft (717 m)
Difficulty: Moderately easy to view;
   loop over mountain adds 410 vertical feet and a steep descent
Maps: Page 144; Trail Conference Map 44 (E-6);
   USGS Arena 7.5' and Lewbeach 7.5'

Summary: Climb on easy grades through a variety of landscapes to an excellent view of Touchmenot Mountain and the Little Pond area from a high open meadow near a pond and an old property foundation.

▶ **Access to area:** From NY 17 (Quickway), exit 96 at Livingston Manor, take the first two right turns. Proceed 0.3 mi and take right turn immediately past Kings Catering. Travel 14.0 mi on County Routes 151, 152, and 54 (same road) to Barkaboom Road. Turn left over bridge for 0.2 mi to Little Pond state campground. From NY 28/30 in Margaretville, travel west to old NY 30, turn left (where NY 28/30 curves right) along the south side of Pepacton Reservoir to Barkaboom Road. Turn left and continue for several miles to campground, right.

Parking and trailhead: Follow campground road for 0.9 mi to a parking area 0.1 mi beyond the tollbooth. From north end of parking area, walk between the showers and bathhouse to a trail register at the rear of the bathhouse. Walk left, following yellow trail markers. ◀

The trail circles around Little Pond, passing near campsites. As you walk next to the pond, note the myriad tree-chewings of beavers. After crossing a bridge at the inlet, you soon come to evidence of past beaver activity at a large beaver meadow. A side path goes right over the old beaver dam. Back on the yellow trail, you enter a lovely conifer forest.

The woods road continues uphill through deciduous woods, meadows, next to pine forests, and past an old shack up in the woods and a stone wall. At 1.3 mi, a path leads left to a muddy pond where turtles bask in the middle and salamanders play in the shallows. Back on the trail, note a stone foundation, slightly obscured, to the right. This is a perfect spot to have had a homestead, at the entry to an extensive open meadow with wonderful views of nearby Touchmenot Mountain and beyond. You can decide whether you want to climb 2760-foot Touchmenot Mountain, too wooded for good viewing, to complete the loop or return the way you came.

To complete the loop, continue across the meadow, ascending through fern-filled woods and climbing to the junction of the red-marked Touchmenot Trail in 0.2 mi. Turn right for 0.8 mi to the summit. As you hike toward Touchmenot

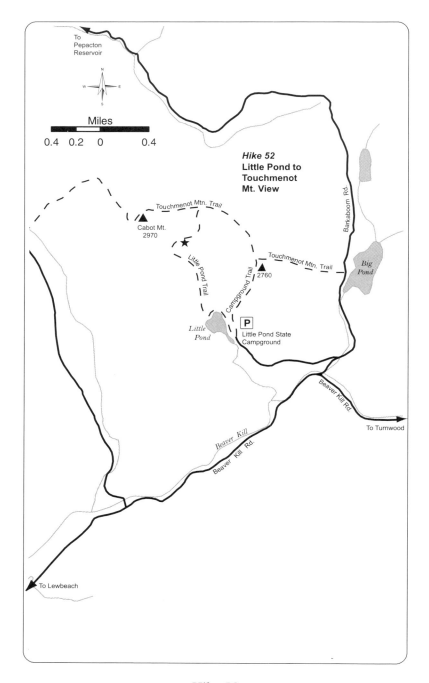

To
Pepacton
Reservoir

N
W E
S

Miles

0.4 0.2 0   0.4

Hike 52
Little Pond to
Touchmenot
Mt. View

Touchmenot Mtn. Trail

Cabot Mt.
2970

★

Little Pond Trail

Campground Trail

Touchmenot Mtn. Trail

2760

Barkaboom Rd.

Big
Pond

Little
Pond

P Little Pond State
Campground

Beaver Kill Rd.

To Turnwood

Beaver Kill

Beaver Kill Rd.

To Lewbeach

Hike 52

Mountain, you pass interesting rock areas that deserve exploration. Be sure to check out the squeeze between rocks at left, partway up. Enormous sedimentary boulders create a walk between rock walls. At 0.5 mi the trail reaches a junction. Avoid the trail, left, which heads east toward Big Pond. Continue straight 0.3 mi with blue markers to the wooded summit, which has very limited views down to Little Pond. Soon you begin a 0.8-mile steep descent, losing altitude rapidly through cuts in rock outcrops. Take care not to hurry, for loose stones can throw you off balance on such steep grades. About halfway down, the descent moderates.

53. Mongaup Pond and Mountain

Round-trip distance: 3.2 mi (5.2 km); loop option, 9.8 mi (15.8 km)
Elevation change: 850 ft (259 m)
Summit elevation: 2989 ft (911 m)
Difficulty: Easy to end of pond; moderate to summit
Maps: Page 146; Trail Conference Map 43 (F-7); USGS Willowemoc 7.5′

Summary: This is the beginning of the 6.4-mile Mongaup-Hardenburgh Trail, which passes over two of Mongaup Mountain's three summits and over Beaver Kill Ridge. All high points are wooded, so viewing is limited until the leaves are off in autumn.

▶ **Access to area:** From NY 17 (Quickway) take exit 96 at Livingston Manor and turn left on County Route 81/82. Proceed 6.0 mi to Debruce. Turn left on Mongaup Road for 3.9 mi to the Mongaup Pond Public Campground. From the tollbooth, bear left to Areas D, E, F, and G for 1.1 mi to a T junction at Areas G–F. Turn left into Area G.

Parking and trailhead: A new parking area is located between sites 151 and 153. Turn right into a gravel pit. The trailhead is just before site 147 on the drive in, at a sign "Trail," 0.2 mi into Area G. ◀

The trail heads toward Mongaup Pond, following blue trail markers. It is also a red-marked snowmobile trail. You parallel the shoreline of beautiful Mongaup Pond to its north end. At a junction with the Mongaup-Hardenburgh Trail, turn left on this blue-marked trail to the register. It is another 1.3 mi to the wooded middle summit of 2989-foot Mongaup Mountain, 800 ft above Mongaup Pond.

This is a scenic woods hike, passing old-growth trees and winding through lovely ferns on a soft trail. The climb is gradual with short, moderate pitches. After the trail turns left, you enter an area of blowdown so extensive that it must have been caused by a microburst, a violent downdraft phenomenon that cuts through areas with tornado-like effects. The clearing here allows a glimpse back

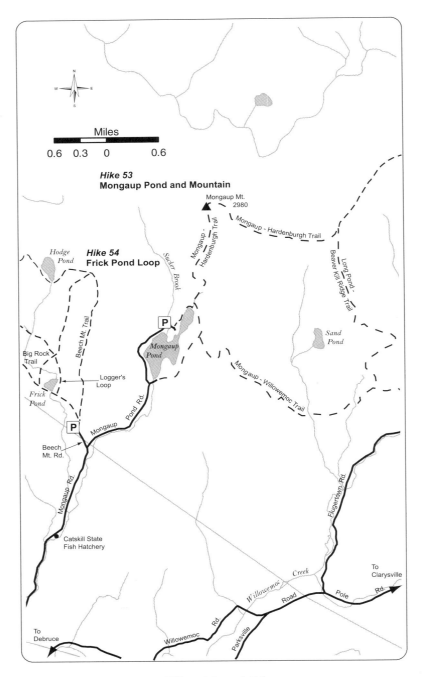

Miles

0.6   0.3   0   0.6

Hike 53
Mongaup Pond and Mountain

Mongaup Mt.
2980

Mongaup – Hardenburgh Trail

Hodge Pond

Hike 54
Frick Pond Loop

Mongaup – Hardenburgh Trail

Stucker Brook

Long Pond – Beaver Kill Ridge Trail

Beech Mt. Trail

P

Mongaup Pond

Sand Pond

Big Rock Trail

Logger's Loop

Frick Pond

Mongaup – Willowemoc Trail

P

Mongaup Pond Rd.

Beech Mt. Rd.

Mongaup Rd.

Flugertown Rd.

Catskill State Fish Hatchery

Creek

To Clarysville

Willowemoc   Road

Pole   Rd.

To Debruce

Willowemoc   Rd.

Parksville   Rd.

Hikes 53 and 54

down at Mongaup Pond.

A couple of steeper but short pitches brings you to the wooded summit at a boulder at 1.6 mi. Before retracing, continue about 100 yds down the trail to see interesting rock ledges. If you're camping here, you may enjoy an extended hike through this beautiful forest.

By adding another half-day, 8.0 more miles, you can combine several trails and hike a sizeable loop back to the trailhead. You'll ascend 1700 ft throughout the hike. Continue east along the Mongaup-Hardenburgh Trail. The trail's only bad footing is on the 400-foot descent in 0.4 mi on leaf-obscured loose rocks to the col between the mountain's summits. The footing beyond the col is very good, regaining 340 ft to the wooded east summit and another 230 ft on the ascent to Beaver Kill Ridge. It's 1.6 mi from Mongaup Mountain's initial summit, 3.2 mi from the start of the trail.

Turn right on the red-marked Long Pond–Beaver Kill Ridge Trail for 2.6 mi. Soon there is a partial view, east. The pretty woods trail descends very gradually. The trail turns south and descends a spur of Beaver Kill Ridge. Just before the trail curves around a ledge, look for a tiny path over to a separated section of cliff overlooking the forest far below.

The trail descends a series of pitches and swings west on gradual grades along the hillside through attractive terrain to the junction of the yellow-marked Mongaup-Willowemoc snowmobile trail. Turn right for 2.9 mi back to Mongaup Pond, climbing a 400-foot ridge! Turn right at the snowmobile trail and circle back around the pond to the trailhead. The parking area is to the right.

This loop can be hiked either way. In reverse, enter Area B, turn right at site 38, and follow the red-marked snowmobile trail. Turn left at the T junction and follow the snowmobile trail north for about 0.8 mi to the Mongaup-Willowemoc Trail junction. Turn right on the yellow-marked trail for 2.8 mi, turn left on the red-marked Long Pond–Beaver Ridge Trail, and left again on the blue-marked Mongaup-Hardenburgh Trail. This will take you back to the pond. Turn left and follow the snowmobile trail back to Area B parking lot.

54. Frick Pond Loop

Round-trip distance: 2.2 mi (3.5 km)
Elevation change: Minor ups and downs
Difficulty: Easy
Maps: Page 146; Trail Conference Map 43 (E-7); USGS Willowemoc 7.5'

Summary: A loop near Mongaup Pond Public Campground, combining parts of three trails with a variety of features, including several bridges, a boardwalk, magnificent conifer forest, mossy wetland, deciduous woods, grassy lane, meadow, and of course, pond.

▶ **Access to area:** From NY 17 (Quickway) exit 96 at Livingston Manor, turn left on County Route 81/82 and proceed 6.0 mi to Debruce. Turn north on Mongaup Road toward Mongaup Pond Public Campground. Follow the Frick Pond Trailhead sign at a fork, left, on Beech Mountain Road at 2.7 mi.

Parking and trailhead: Travel 0.4 mi to a large parking area left. Follow red DEC trail markers down steps from the northwest corner of the parking lot. ◀

A trail register is located at 0.1 mi. Continue left along the woods road. As the straight trail heads toward Frick Pond, look for stately old-growth white pines. The remains of an old homestead with rusting bunk beds appear left above the wildflowers. There is a nearby memorial off the trail. At 0.4 mi, the Loggers Trail bears right where you return after the loop. For now, continue straight on the red-marked trail, descending to the shore at 0.5 mi. You may want to go to the pond's shore here, because the trail does not approach the pond later.

Cross the 50-foot bridge at the pond's outlet, bear right, and climb a small grade overlooking the pond. After a second bridge crossing, take the Big Rock Trail, right, at the junction, following yellow markers. Circling some distance from the pond, you enter a lovely grove of large hemlock and more handsome old-growth white pine. A wide, 285-foot raised boardwalk over lush sphagnum moss takes you to two bridges over the inlets to Frick Pond.

The trail heads northeast to Times Square, a four-way junction (not nearly as bustling as its namesake). Turn right onto the cross-country ski trail called the Loggers Trail, and ascend a gradual grade where partial views right to Frick Pond appear through the woods. The trail crosses an open field and rejoins the Quick Lake Trail you came in on.

This is a terrific area for cross-country skiing, with many connecting trails.

55. Covered Bridge Trek to Waterfall

Round-trip distance: About 1.0 mi (1.6 km)
Elevation change: Minor ascent
Difficulty: Easy
Maps: Page 149; USGS Willowemoc 7.5'

Summary: A short walk up an unmarked path to a lovely waterfall near public and private campgrounds. This is an ideal spot to cool off on a hot day. There is fishing access on the Willowemoc River.

▶ **Access to area:** From NY 17 (Quickway) exit 96 at Livingston Manor, turn left

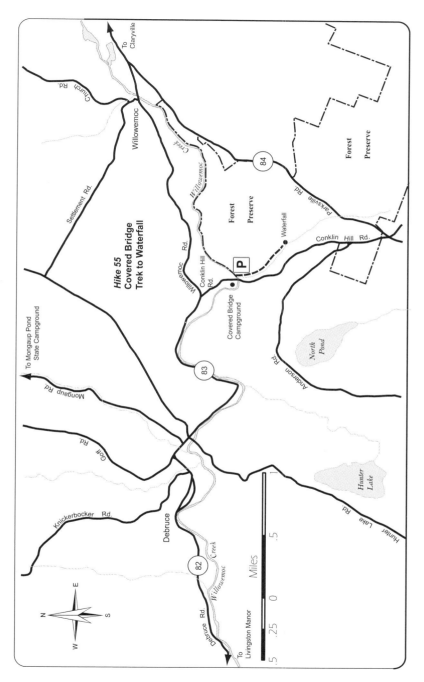

Hike 55
Covered Bridge
Trek to Waterfall

Hike 55

on County Route 81/82 to Debruce. Continue east past Mongaup Road to Conklin Hill Road and turn right; pass Covered Bridge Campground and cross the covered bridge. From NY 17 at Parksville, turn north on County Route 85/84 to Conklin Hill Road (opposite Aden Hill Road). Turn north on Conklin Hill Road and bear right at the fork, continuing down to the covered bridge.

Parking and trailhead: Park just south of the bridge is an area that accommodates three to four cars. To the right, follow the unmarked path away from the Willowemoc River, heading south. ◀

Paths along the Willowemoc Creek invite later exploration. For now, head south to the waterfall, following the path right of the small tributary stream that flows into the Willowemoc Creek. Several yards upstream, the path crosses the stream on slippery rocks, so be cautious.

Before long you arrive at a nice first waterfall. The path continues upstream, sometimes climbing the bank, past a second small falls to large, cliff-like ledges on the left. Beyond, a beautiful large waterfall drops into a shallow pool, enabling the hiker to wade under the sunny spray on a hot day. Bring wading sneakers and test for slippery footing.

This is a fine short excursion if you are camping in this popular area.

56. Split Rock Lookout

Round-trip distance: 3.0 mi (4.8 km)
Elevation change: 600 ft (183 m)
High-point elevation: 2500 ft (762 m)
Difficulty: Moderate. *Note:* Tropical Storm Irene washed out first 0.4 mi (2011)
Maps: Page 152; Trail Conference Map 44 (B-6); USGS Downsville 7.5' and Lewbeach 7.5'

Summary: This hike offers a fine variety of landscapes: an old beaver pond, an impressive old-growth spruce and red pine forest, and a climb to the top of a cliff. The cliff top rewards the hiker with a large rock perch, separated from the cliff, for viewing the countryside.

▶ **Access to area:** From the west on NY 30 (south of Pepacton Reservoir), turn south on NY 206 for 5.0 mi. Turn east on Little Spring Brook Road (cutoff), and left at a T-intersection, continuing to the end, less than a mi. From the south on NY 17 in Roscoe, travel 6.2 mi north on NY 206. Turn east on Little Spring Brook Road (main entrance) and continue 1.1 mi to its end.

Parking and trailhead: Park in area on the right before the grassy lawn of a small hunting lodge at road's end. The trail begins across the lawn. ◀

Plan to hike this trail after a dry period, for the first 0.2 mi is potentially muddy from stream runoff. The old lane, with yellow markers, is rocky at first, but improves steadily as you progress. Crossing a culvert at 0.3 mi, the trail becomes drier and less rocky. Soon, you see an old beaver pond ahead. If you're quiet, you may see a great blue heron and other wildlife activity.

Beyond, the trail enters state land in a lovely spruce, red pine, and maple forest. The lane is now of drivable quality, with excellent footing. The ascent is gradual up to a junction in a clearing at 0.7 mi. Turn right on the blue-marked Pelnor Hollow Trail. Soon you cross a brook and enter a magnificent plantation of huge spruce, red pine, and scotch pine. The walk through the shady rows of great trees on soft, needle-covered terrain next to a mossy rivulet is wonderful.

The trail enters a deciduous woods and a rerouted trail swings north and east to climb to the cliff top on moderate grades. If you see markers heading straight toward the cliff through a wet area, you can climb very steeply and save an extra 0.3 mi, but the longer route is recommended for the descent! Following the new route up, the trail gradually swings south and heads along the top of the cliff to a short spur path, right, marked by a tank-shaped boulder at the end. Your destination is this excellent lookout ledge, now called Split Rock Lookout.

Caution! Approach the edge of this cliff with care; a very deep crevice separates the lookout ledge from the rest of the hillside. Go left around a huge boulder, known as a glacial erratic, and carefully descend to a spot where you can step over to the large ledge. Here, also, the crevice is deep, but it is a small step over to the ledge. Obviously, children should be kept close at this interesting spot. Fine views are seen to the north and west.

57. Mary Smith Hill

Round-trip distance: eastern approach, 4.2 mi (16.8 km); western approach, 2.3 mi (3.7 km)
Elevation change: From the east, 800 ft (244 m);
   from the west, 600 ft (183 m)
High-point elevation: eastern approach, 2900 ft (884 m);
   western approach, 2700 ft (823 m)
Difficulty: Moderate overall, but very steep sections
Maps: Page 152; Trail Conference Map 44 (C-6); USGS Lewbeach 7.5'

Summary: Part of the Delaware Ridge Trail, the Mary Smith Trail offers surprisingly steep ascents for this "hill" country, with two nice lookouts. Here's a spot to get some serious exercise in an off-the-beaten-track area between Little Pond and Beaverkill Campgrounds, both public. (Note that access to the western

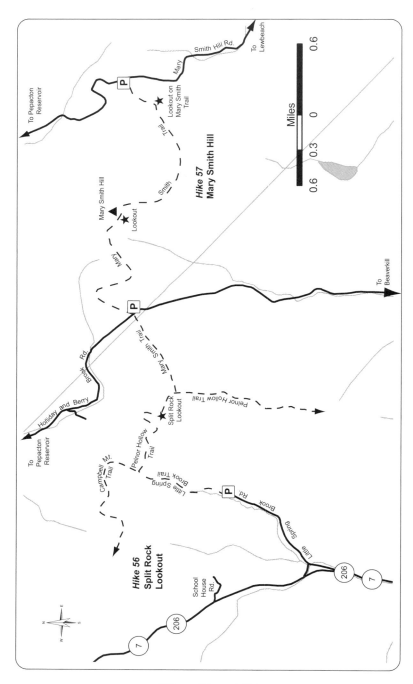

Hikes 56 and 57

approach is on a higher quality road.)

Access to area: Eastern approach: Turn north 3.2 mi on Mary Smith Hill Road from Lewbeach, 10 mi north of Livingston Manor on County Route 151/152. From Little Pond Campground, travel 0.2 mi south, turning right on County Route 54/152 to Lewbeach. From Beaverkill Campground, take County Route 152 north to Lewbeach. From the north on NY 30, turn south on Beech Hill Road for 1.1 mi. Fork right onto Mary Smith Hill Road at 2.2 mi.

Western approach: Travel approximately 5.0 mi north from the Beaverkill Campground covered bridge on Holliday and Berry Brook Road. From NY 30, travel south for about 2.5 mi.

Parking and trailhead: Mary Smith Hill Road (eastern) approach: The parking area is on the east side of the road at the height of land, and is marked by DEC signs. The Mary Smith Trail is across the road, heading west.

Holliday and Berry Brook Road (western) approach: Park on the east side of the road. The trail register is in a large clearing, and your trail starts on this side of the road.

Eastern approach: If you hike this trail in early May (before blackfly season), you'll enjoy a profusion of wildflowers. Spring beauties, Dutchman's breeches, yellow violets, trout lilies, and red trillium abound on the sloping hillside.

Leaving the trailhead, the terrain soon steepens and remains steep until a switchback, left, gives a momentary breather. All too soon you begin scrambling up an eroded section, but it is short. The grade becomes more moderate here and reaches mossy ledges. You have the feeling of arriving at a high point, and at 0.5 mi, the trail takes you to a flat rock overlooking the southern valley, a great place to rest.

Resume on level terrain briefly before ascending another 200 vertical feet near the area's high point at 2,942 ft, 0.9 mi from the trailhead. The path gradually loses elevation as it turns northwest on the ridge. If leaves are off the trees—the best time to hike these wooded ridges—you can view the nearby hills.

Mary Smith Hill is 175 ft lower than the high point you passed, so the next 1.2 mi is a very gradual descent across the ridge connecting these hills. This trek is a delightful contrast to the rigor of the first mile! After the trail has crossed the ridge and is following the southern edge of the hillside, look for a well-worn short path past a boulder at 2.1 mi. Surrounded by interesting mossy ledges, this spot offers a fine view toward the Beaverkill Valley.

(Back at the Mary Smith Hill Road trailhead, the trail to "Middle Mountain Vista" is misnamed. Unless you hike when the leaves are down, the view is obscured by tall trees growing close together on the ledges. Nonetheless, it's a nice trail through open deciduous woods and ascents to the top of rocky outcrops, with places to poke around at 0.5 mi. The "vista" is 0.6 mi farther.)

Western approach. This shorter approach ascends most of Mary Smith Hill in the first half of the hike and is therefore even steeper than the approach from the east. The ascent starts soon and does not abate for about 0.5 mi. One section challenges the hiker to stay upright, and indeed on the descent it may be impossible to do so. Avoid this approach after wet or icy weather, although with ample packable snow, the ascents are possible and the descents are great slides.

The rewards of this trail are worth the labor. It becomes mostly level after 0.5 mi. Occasional pitches upward pass through scenic mossy ledges, fine examples of sedimentary buildup over the millennia.

At 1.0 mi, go off-trail along the top of a large ledge. You can look many feet down into a natural fortress-like formation. In another 0.2 mi, look for the short path by a boulder to an expansive view to the south.

These trails have many berry brambles, so wear or bring long pants—and bring a container for berries in midsummer!

58. Trout Pond and Mud Pond

Round-trip distances: Trout Pond, 2.8 mi (4.5 km); Mud Pond, 2.0 mi (3.2 km); loop, 4.7 mi (7.6 km)
Elevation change: Trout Pond, 300 ft (91 m); Mud Pond, 350 ft (107 m);
   loop, 750 ft (229 m)
Difficulty: Moderately easy
Maps: Page 155; Trail Conference Map 44 (A-7);
   USGS Roscoe 7.5' and Downsville 7.5'

Summary: This area offers fishing and informal camping areas near remote, undeveloped ponds. The 4.7-mile loop involves a climb of 750 ft. (Ascending separately to each pond is less total ascent.) Russell Brook is a public fishing area with an attractive waterfall upstream from the trailhead bridge.

▶ **Access to area:** From Butternut Grove on NY 17, travel 3.5 mi north on Russell Brook Road. From Roscoe on NY 17, take NY 206 north for 2.4 mi to Morton Hill Road, just past the Beaver Kill bridge. Turn west (bearing right in 0.2 mi) for 3.0 mi to Russell Brook Road (unmarked). Turn left for 0.5 mi.

Parking and trailhead: From Butternut Grove, it is the second parking area on the left. From Roscoe, it is the first area (right). ◀

Although you can ascend either way, the loop heads to Trout Pond first. The trail descends beyond the gated roadway and crosses a bridge over Russell Brook. Across a meadow are sections of an old stone bridge with a pretty waterfall beyond. A trail register at 0.1 mi is opposite a campsite on a grassy rise to the

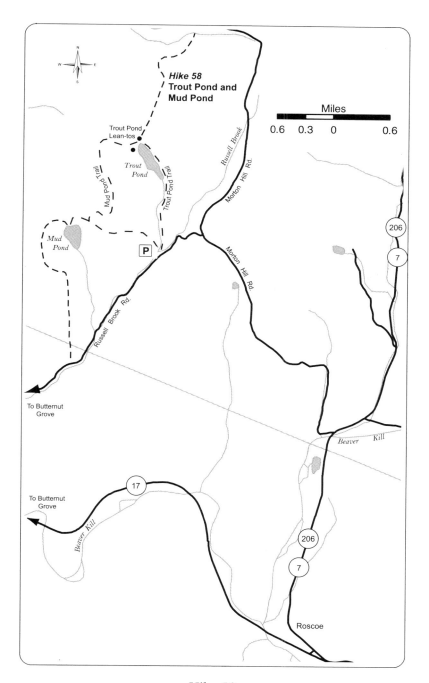

Hike 58
Trout Pond and Mud Pond

Miles

0.6   0.3   0   0.6

Trout Pond
Lean-tos

Trout Pond

Mud Pond Trail

Trout Pond Trail

Russell Brook

Morton Hill Rd.

P

Mud Pond

Morton Hill Rd.

Russell Brook Rd.

To Butternut Grove

206

7

Beaver Kill

17

To Butternut Grove

Beaver Kill

206

7

Roscoe

Hike 58

right. Other campsites are located a few yards left along the Mud Pond Trail.

At the junction, continue straight (right) to Trout Pond up an old woods road for 0.8 mi, a gradual and then moderate ascent of 300 ft. Signs for informal campsites are posted in areas to the left between the trail and the outlet stream. Trout Pond, also known as Cables Lake, offers excellent fishing, and its popularity can cause a litter problem. Frogs, pollywogs, and salamanders abound as you hike 0.5 mi along the east side of this sizable body of water.

Soon after passing a small dam, you reach a junction at the north end of the pond near a lean-to. If you want to climb 450 ft up Cherry Ridge (2500 ft elevation, no views) to hike the loop to Mud Pond, turn left on the blue-marked Mud Pond Trail and cross the Trout Pond inlet bridge.

The trail winds below the ledges of the ridge top and swings south to a height of land at 0.8 mi, then gradually descends along a stream (which can be dry) on rocky footing. After passing through an interesting stand of tiny trees and reaching a junction at 1.9 mi from the Trout Pond junction, turn right. In about 0.1 mi turn left to a well-worn path to Mud Pond. Note a large, open campsite right, with chairs made of rocks. At this isolated pond, you might see trails tunneling into grass from the water—a nearby beaver lodge signals the source of this activity.

Return to the trail and retrace, right, back to the junction. Continue straight ahead up a rise, then descend steadily on a wide trail with good footing through attractive forest for 0.9 mi to the junction where you began the loop. Turn right back to Russell Brook and up to the trailhead.

"The place to observe nature is where you are."

—JOHN BURROUGHS

Northwest Catskills

The mountains and streams of the northwest Catskills nourished naturalist and writer John Burroughs, who was born in Roxbury and attended a one-room schoolhouse there. Burroughs acquired most of his education through his own efforts, however, developing acute powers of observation and appreciation from this wild region. In subsequent years, special editions of some of his thirty books on nature were required reading in schools and colleges across the United States.

Along with soul mates Ralph Waldo Emerson, Henry David Thoreau, and John Muir, Burroughs believed that regular retreat to the natural world is the catalyst for a return to simplicity and reverence: "The most precious things of life are near at hand, without money and without price. Each of you has the whole wealth of the universe at your very door."

Although he counted the rich and famous among his friends, Burroughs never forgot his Catskill upbringing. "I have shared the common lot," he wrote, "and it is good enough for me." The John Burroughs Memorial Field (see below) is a testament to regional pride in Burroughs's Catskill roots.

This part of the Catskills, once a major center for the tanning industry, is now known for winter sports and the arts.

If you have time after a hike, want a change of pace, or the weather isn't cooperating, consider one of the following attractions:

John Burroughs Memorial Field. Just yards from his boyhood home, this site celebrates the life of the renowned naturalist and writer John Burroughs (1837–1921), whose love of wilderness permeates all his works. The location offers a pictorial display commemorating Burroughs's youth, his early and long marriage, his many friendships with "movers and shakers" of his time, and his writings on the everyday miracle of the natural world. A path at right leads a few yards to Boyhood Rock, which offers a beautiful view of his childhood surroundings. From there, an informal path ascends into woods for about a half-mile, circling around a hillside and leading to a clearing with additional views. Woodchuck Lodge, Burroughs's homestead, is the cabin situated a few hundred feet down the road from the memorial field. A short loop (0.5 mi round-trip) right of the cabin ascends log and stone steps. (Note: The loop stays at rear of Woodchuck Lodge area.) North of Roxbury on NY 30, turn west on Hardscrabble Road (north of the hamlet of Hubbell Corners). At 0.9 mi, turn left on John Burroughs Memorial Road and proceed to the field at 1.4 mi. Park on the side of the road.

Schoharie Reservoir Dam. Gilboa. From NY 30 north of Grand Gorge, turn east on County Route 990V to viewing platform. For the Gorge, continue 2.0 mi through Gilboa to new bridge.

Mine Kill Falls. Spectacular gorge with trail to overlook platform. Take NY 30 for 8.0 mi north of Grand Gorge.

Red Falls. Unsupervised swimming in a large natural pool and cascades on the Batavia Creek, NY 23, between Ashland and Prattsville. Swim at your own risk. Diving should not be attempted.

Zadock Pratt Museum. Restored home of tanning industry pioneer and states-man (see Hike 60), Pratt Rock Park. Wed.–Sun., 1–5 P.M., Main St., Prattsville, NY. 518-299-3395.

59. Bearpen Mountain

Round-trip distance: 9.0 mi (14.5 km), west summit
Elevation change: 1600 ft (488 m)
Summit elevation: 3600 ft (1098 m)
Difficulty: Moderately strenuous. Steady ascent on an old road,
   then gradual and level lane to final short, steep ascent.
Maps: Page 159; USGS Prattsville 7.5'

Summary: A long round-trip to a summit with good views and no difficult ascents, despite its status as one of the thirty-five Catskill peaks over 3500 ft. From the summit there are excellent views north and northeast and down to the Schoharie Valley.

▷ **Access to area:** From NY 23 in Prattsville, immediately north of the Schoharie Creek Bridge, turn south on County Route 2 for 2.0 mi. Just beyond Peckham Road, look for a grassy lane heading into the woods on the right. This is the unmarked "Ski Run Road," barely discernible in the trees. It is at the hilltop, across from a meadow, with great views to Bearpen.

   Parking and trailhead: Park in the clearing at the beginning of "Ski Run Road". ◁

Like fifteen of the other Catskill high peaks that exceed 3500 ft, Bearpen is offi-cially trailless, so there are no markers. Jeep roads lead to the summit of this old ski area, so the route is easy to follow. (Bearpen has been acquired by New York State, so changes may be made.)

   Gradual grades up the lane take you through attractive woods by stone walls. The terrain drops off on the left as the road slabs up the hillside, affording views

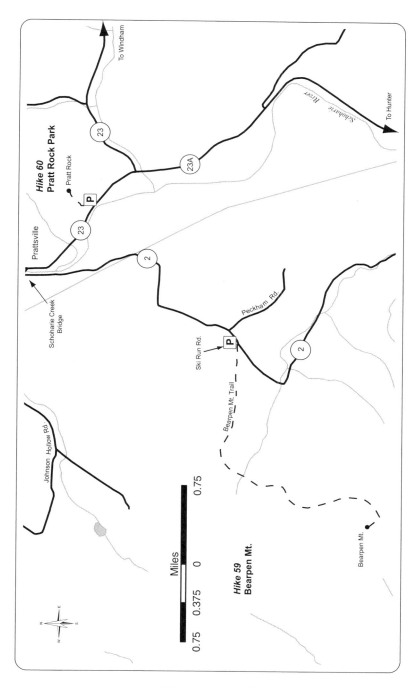

To Windham

23

Hike 60
Pratt Rock Park

Pratt Rock

P

Prattsville

23

Schoharie River

23A

To Hunter

Schoharie Creek
Bridge

2

Peckham Rd.

P

Ski Run Rd.

2

Bearpen Mt. Trail

Johnson Hollow Rd.

Bearpen Mt.

N
E
S
W

Miles

0.75   0.375   0   0.75

Hike 59
Bearpen Mt.

Hikes 59 and 60

through the trees to the long summit ridge of Bearpen. Views are especially nice in winter through bare trees. The grade steepens on rocky road above what we called "rubble without a cause" to a hunter's camp in 2.4 mi. Do not follow the lane right of the camp, but go left and follow the mostly level old road toward Bearpen for 1.5 mi. Sections are rutted with big puddles, so choose a dry period for optimal conditions. Generally, the footing is excellent above the camp.

When the road seems to end suddenly at 3.9 mi, the trail turns right and circles around the area. There are "Posted" signs, but continue on the trail which swings around left back to the road, where you turn right. (If you turn left over a dirt mound soon after the diversion right, continue straight along the road.) Note these features for your return trip, because this is a short but confusing area.

After a pond on the right at 4.2 mi, a final short downgrade leads to the former ski area. Raspberry bushes abound on this mountainside. You can continue on the road below the final upgrade to a fork, right, through woods and bear right up to the east summit. Or you can turn right immediately, climbing steeply up a path. A ledge at the top affords a view, looking back.

In winter, this steep path up to the west summit is a good choice because excellent views west and south can be had from this side of Bearpen. At the top of the path, carefully walk right to the rock ledge, an excellent winter overlook. Exercise caution around the cliff-like drop-offs in this area.

Follow the main path along the level summit to the overlook clearing, left, with excellent views of Hunter Mountain, Kaaterskill High Peak far east, Windham High Peak, Roundtop Mountain (one of three so named in the region) near to the northwest, and the ridge of your ascent route. With binoculars you can discern the white blazes on Pratt Rock, directly across the valley. The two summit clearings are connected by a path, allowing you to explore and enjoy both overlook areas.

Bearpen's broad summit is especially nice in winter with the foliage off, more like an open summit when you are standing on many feet of snow. Moderate and level grades make the route a fine snowshoe or ski.

60. Pratt Rock Park

Round-trip distance: 1.0 mi (1.6 km)
Elevation change: About 200 ft (61 m)
Difficulty: Moderately easy; short, but steep
Maps: Page 159; USGS Prattsville 7.5'

Summary: This short climb through the 20-acre park takes you nearly 200 years back into American history to a memorial celebrating Zadock Pratt, a local businessman and statesman from Schoharieskill. Owing to his influence, the town was later referred to as the "gem of the Catskills." The citizenry changed the village name to Prattsville in 1833.

▶ **Access to area:** On NY 23 just east of Prattsville, 0.4 mi west of the junction of NY 23 and NY 23A.

Parking and trailhead: A parking area is just east of the steps leading up to an exhibit. ◀

Pratt Rock, listed in the State Register of Historic Places, begins at a covered exhibit area, with much of historic interest. A great deal of the original Catskill forest was hemlock, the bark of which contained the tannin needed for tanning leather. In the early 19th century, Zadock Pratt's enterprise tanned a million hides in twenty years. Prattsville became the largest tannery in the world, clearing 10,000 acres of hemlock.

Colonel Zadock Pratt converted the town into one of the first planned communities in the early 1800s, re-routing the road, building a dam, constructing many homes, stores, and sidewalks, and planting hundreds of trees. The town had three tanneries, four textile factories, three gristmills, many schools, churches, and hotels, and a bank opened by Pratt. The printed currency had his own name on it.

Pratt became a U.S. Congressman in 1836, founded the National Bureau of Statistics, was involved in the construction of the Washington Monument, and introduced the Postage Act, which lowered postage rates from a quarter to a nickel. The Pratt Tannery closed by 1846, after the hemlock had been completely harvested. Farming became the chief industry.

A path winds quite steeply up a terraced picnic area, past a monument commemorating one of Pratt's favorite horses (he owned over a thousand horses in his lifetime). Climbing into woods, you soon arrive at the base of the cliff. Into it are sculptured white-washed figures and writings illustrating Pratt's life through symbols: a hemlock, a horse, Pratt's face, his son George killed in the Civil War, the family motto and shield, an uplifted hand (the symbol of the 20th State Militia), and an arm and hammer representing the working person, whom Pratt held in great regard.

Much open rock allows expansive views of the Schoharie Valley from the top of the cliff. Do not continue beyond the displays, but retrace to a side path, climbing to the right under the horse, to ascend.

Appendix A

Route Difficulty at a Glance

Easy
Alder Lake, Hike 51 (p. 142)
Ashokan Reservoir, Hike 33 (p. 101)
Becker Hollow, Hike 20 (p. 73)
Catskill Mountain House and Lakeside Loop, Hike 8 (p. 47)
Covered Bridge Trek to Waterfall, Hike 55 (p. 148)
Diamond Notch Falls, Hike 19 (p. 72)
Frick Pond Loop, Hike 54 (p. 147)
Onteora Lake, Hike 32 (p. 98)
Rider Hollow Trail, Hike 37 (p. 109)
Seager Trail to Waterfalls, Hike 38 (p. 111)

Moderately easy. Involves ascents, occasionally steep
Boulder Rock and Split Rock Loop, Hike 2 (p. 34)
Cathedral Glen Loop, Hike 35 (p. 106)
Dutcher Notch from Colgate Lake, Hike 15 (p. 61)
Echo Lake and Overlook Mountain from Platte Clove, Hike 30 (p. 94)
Inspiration Point and Hudson River Valley Lookout, Hike 1 (p. 33)
Kaaterskill Falls, Hike 7 (p. 46)
Kelly Hollow, Hike 40 (p. 115)
Little Pond to Touchmenot Mountain View, Hike 52 (p. 143)
Magical Quarry on Sugarloaf, Hike 23 (p. 77)
Pratt Rock Park, Hike 60 (p. 160)
Red Hill, Hike 48 (p. 133)
Sunset Rock and Newmans Ledge, Hike 3 (p. 36)
Trout Pond and Mud Pond, Hike 58 (p. 154)
Vernooy Kill Falls, Hike 49 (p. 135)

Moderate. Requires strenuous effort, only occasional steep ascents
Acra Point and Burnt Knob, Hike 12 (p. 55)
Balsam Lake Mountain Loop, Hike 50 (p. 140)
Biscuit Brook Bushwhack, Hike 47 (p. 131)
Colonels Chair Trail to Hunter Summit, Hike 18 (p. 71)
Diamond Notch, Hike 19 (p. 72)
Giant Ledge, Hike 42 (p. 122)
Huckleberry Point, Hike 27 (p. 87)

Lookouts on Dry Brook Ridge, Hike 39 (p. 113)
Mary Smith Hill, Hike 57 (p. 151)
Mongaup Pond and Mountain, Hike 53 (p. 145)
North Point Loop, Hike 4 (p. 38)
Overlook Mountain from Woodstock, Hike 29 (p. 91)
Palenville Overlook from South Lake, Hike 6 (p. 43)
Rochester Hollow, Hike 36 (p. 108)
Sleepy Hollow Trail to Little Pine Orchard Picnic Area, Hike 5 (p. 42)
Split Rock Lookout, Hike 56 (p. 150)

**Moderately strenuous. Steep areas or steady grades,
with significant overall ascent**
Bearpen Mountain, Hike 59 (p. 158)
Belleayre Mountain, Hike 34 (p. 104)
Camels Hump, Hike 11 (p. 53)
Hunter Mountain from Spruceton Valley, Hike 17 (p. 67)
Mount Tremper from Willow, Hike 31 (p. 96)
Palenville Overlook from Palenville, Hike 6 (p. 43)
Peekamoose Trail to Overlook Ledge, Hike 45 (p. 126)
Slide Mountain Loop via Curtis-Ormsbee Trail, Hike 41 (p. 120)
Windham High Peak, Hike 13 (p. 56)

Strenuous. Steep ascents and great overall elevation change
Ashokan High Point, Hike 46 (p. 129)
Balsam Mountain Loop, Hike 37 (p. 109)
Black Dome Mountain, Hike 9 (p. 49)
Blackhead Mountain Loop, Hike 10 (p. 52)
Hunter Mountain from Stony Clove, Hike 17 (p. 67)
Kaaterskill High Peak, Hike 26 (p. 86)
Orchard Point and Dannys Lookout, Hike 21 (p. 74)
Poets Ledge and Wildcat Falls, Hike 28 (p. 89)
Stoppel Point, Hike 14 (p. 59)
West Kill Mountain, Hike 16 (p. 64)

Difficult. Involves extremely steep areas
Indian Head Mountain Loop, Hike 25 (p. 81)
Sugarloaf Mountain Loop, Hike 22 (p. 75)
Twin Mountain from Pecoy Notch and Jimmy Dolan Notch, Hike 24 (p. 78)
Wittenberg–Cornell–Slide Mountain Loop from Woodland Valley, Hike 44 (p. 125)
Wittenberg Mountain, Hike 43 (p. 123)

Appendix B

Sources and Resources

Catskill Forest Preserve Information

The Department of Environmental Conservation (DEC) operates all New York State campgrounds within the Forest Preserve. For further information about campgrounds, fishing, hiking, hunting, and other outdoor activities, consult the following:

New York State campgrounds, information only: www.dec.state.ny.us or 518-457-2500

New York State campgrounds, reservations only: www.reserveamerica.com or 800-456-CAMP (456-2267)

To request other information, including DEC publications: www.dec.state.ny.us or 518-402-8013

Or write:
Division of Public Affairs
New York State Department of Environmental Conservation (DEC)
625 Broadway
Albany, NY 12233-4500

The DEC has forest rangers patrolling the trails. For information or assistance, note the following numbers. (For emergencies, see box on page 18.)

DEC Region 3 (Ulster and Sullivan counties)
21 South Putt Corners Road
New Paltz, NY 12561
Forest Rangers: 845-256-3000

DEC Region 4 (Delaware and Greene counties)

Jefferson Road	1150 North Westcott Road
Stamford, NY 12167	Schenectady, NY 12306
Forest Rangers: 607-652-7365	Forest Rangers: 518-357-2234

Other Web sites of interest

Leave No Trace: www.lnt.org
Views from the Top: www.viewsfromthetop.com
Catskill 3500 Club: www.catskill-3500-club.com

Tourism

A nearly endless variety of events are offered throughout the Catskills year-round. These include arts and crafts exhibitions, music festivals, historical museums, Oktoberfests, sporting events, and seasonal attractions. Please contact the following for further information and schedules of events:

General information for the Catskill Region: 800-882-2287.

Office of Public Information, Sullivan County Government Center, Monticello, NY 12701. Telephone: 914-794-3000, ext. 5010.

Ulster County Public Information Office, County Office Bldg., 244 Fair St., P.O. Box 1800, Kingston, NY 12401. Telephone: 800-342-5826.

Greene County Tourism Association, Box 332, Cairo, NY 12413. Telephone: 800-355-CATS.

Delaware County Tourism. 114 Main St., Delhi, NY 13753. Telephone: 800-642-4443, ext. 32.

Weather

Kingston area: 845-331-5555
National Weather Service: www.nws.noaa.gov

Appendix C

Glossary

Bushwhack: Off-trail hiking with map and compass.

Clove: A narrow valley (a ravine, gap, or cleft) created by a river cutting into the ancient Catskill Delta. Between the valleys, or cloves, the remaining plateau outwardly resembles mountains.

Col: A pass or low point between two adjacent mountains.

Escarpment: A long cliff or steep slope separating two comparatively level or more gently sloping surfaces and resulting from erosion or faulting. A tectonic collision formed the mountains of New England, the Appalachian Plateau, and the Catskill Delta. Erosion of soft shales created the Hudson River Valley, while a hard caprock conglomerate protected the softer rock of the Catskill region. The Great Wall of Manitou, rising 1600 feet above the Hudson River Valley, is the eastern scarp of the Catskill region

Herd Path: Unmarked and unmaintained paths created by hikers.

Hollow: A low area surrounded by elevations; a small valley, basin, or channel.

Kill: The Dutch word for waterway, creek, or river. Catskill may have originated from the Dutch ship, *The Kat*, that voyaged up the Hudson shortly before the name came into use. Others believe the name came from Jacob Cats, keeper of the Great Seal of Holland during that period. Katts Kills, the Dutch name for the region, could have been Anglicized to Wild Cat Creek, named after the indigenous bay lynx.

Lean-to: A three-sided shelter with an overhanging roof and one open side.

Notch: A narrow pass created by erosion, which is responsible for the mountainous appearance of the region and explains the characteristic steep rise and flat summits of Catskill peaks. The nearly horizontal rock layers of the uplifted Catskill Delta are unlike the more tilted or folded rock of true mountain ranges.

Post-hole: To sink deeply with each step into snow, a problem usually remedied by the use of snowshoes.

Slab (vb.): When a trail traverses around a mountainside or other sloped area, making footing more difficult than direct ascending or descending.

About the Authors

Residents of central New York, Carol Stone White and David Scott White hike extensively in the Catskills, Adirondacks, New England, and the Finger Lakes region. They write hiking columns for the *Poughkeepsie Journal*'s "My Valley" and the magazine *Catskill Mountain Region Guide*, and their articles have appeared in ADK's *Adirondac* magazine and the *Adirondack Explorer*. Carol edited *Catskill Peak Experiences* and *Adirondack Peak Experiences*, completing the trilogy in 2012 with *Peak Experiences: Danger, Death, and Daring in the Mountains of the Northeast*, published by University Press of New England.

In 1994, Carol and David joined the winter Catskill 3500 Club, whose members climb all thirty-five peaks exceeding 3500 feet. The Whites went on to become Winter Forty-Sixers in 1997, and Carol compiled *Women with Altitude*, which chronicles the lives and adventures of the first thirty-three women to climb the forty-six high peaks in winter. (She is #20.) The couple completed winter climbs of the forty-eight peaks over 4000 feet in the White Mountains and have climbed eight of Colorado's 14,000-footers.

In addition to *Catskill Day Hikes*, the Whites edited *Catskill Trails*, also published by ADK, and assisted in preparation of the National Geographic Trails Illustrated Map #755, *Catskill Park*, published in partnership with the Adirondack Mountain Club. From 2001 to 2003, the Whites hiked 350 miles using a surveyor's wheel to fine-tune trail measurements throughout the Catskills.

The Whites participate in trail maintenance, lead hikes, restore lean-tos, and have taught extended hiking classes. They have served in volunteer leadership positions for ADK, the Adirondack Forty-Sixers, and the Catskill 3500 Club, for which David is now membership chair and Carol conservation committee chair. Carol received the Susan B. Anthony Legacy Award in 2007 with long-distance swimmer Lynne Cox and polar explorer Ann Bancroft.

Dave is former president of Clinton Computer Systems, and Carol former village trustee and chair of the Clinton Planning Board.

Backdoor to Backcountry

ADKers choose from friendly outings, for those just getting started with local chapters, to Adirondack backpacks and international treks. Learn gradually through chapter outings or attend an ADK program. A sampling includes:

- Alpine Flora
- Basic Canoeing/Kayaking
- Bicycle Touring
- Mountain Photography
- Cross-country Skiing and Snowshoeing
- Winter Mountaineering
- Birds of the Adirondacks
- Geology of the High Peaks ... and more!

For more information about the Adirondacks or ADK:
ADK's Information Center & Headquarters, 814 Goggins Rd., Lake George, NY 12845-4117; Tel. 518-668-4447. E-mail: adkinfo@adk.org
Exit 21 off I-87 ("the Northway"), 9N south
Open 8:30 AM–5 PM, Monday–Saturday

For more information about ADK lodges: ADK Lodges, Box 867, Lake Placid, NY 12946; Tel. 518-523-3441, 9:00 AM–7:00 PM. Visit our Web site at www.adk.org

Join Us

We are a nonprofit membership organization that brings together people with interests in recreation, conservation, and environmental education in the New York State Forest Preserve.

Membership Benefits

*   **Discovery:**
    ADK can broaden your horizons by introducing you to new places, recreational activities, and interests.

*   **Enjoyment:**
    Being outdoors more and loving it more.

*   **People:**
    Meeting others and sharing the fun.

*   *Adirondac* **Magazine.**

*   **Member Discounts:**
    20% off on guidebooks, maps, and other ADK publications; discount on lodge stays; 10% discount on educational programs.

*   **Satisfaction:**
    Knowing you're doing your part and that future generations will enjoy the wilderness as you do.

*   **Chapter Participation:**
    Brings you the fun of outings and other social activities and the reward of working on trails, conservation, and education projects at the local level. You can also join as a member at large. Either way, all Club activities and benefits are available.

Membership
To Join

Call **800-395-8080** (Mon.–Sat., 8:30 A.M.–5:00 P.M.), visit **www.adk.org**, or send this form with payment to:

Adirondack Mountain Club
814 Goggins Road
Lake George, NY 12845-4117

Check Membership Level:

☐ Individual $45

☐ Family $55*

☐ Student $35
(full time, 18 and over)

☐ Senior (65 or over) $35

☐ Senior Family $45*

☐ Lifetime Individual $1200

☐ Lifetime Family $1800*

School _____

Includes associate/family members
Fees subject to change.

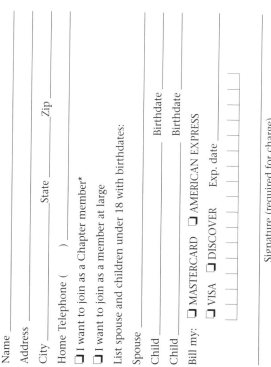

Name _____

Address _____

City _____ State _____ Zip _____

Home Telephone ( ) _____

☐ I want to join as a Chapter member*
☐ I want to join as a member at large

List spouse and children under 18 with birthdates:

Spouse _____

Child _____ Birthdate _____

Child _____ Birthdate _____

Bill my: ☐ MASTERCARD ☐ AMERICAN EXPRESS
       ☐ VISA ☐ DISCOVER   Exp. date _____

☐☐☐☐ ☐☐☐☐ ☐☐☐☐

_____
Signature (required for charge)

* For details, call 800-395-8080 (Mon.–Sat., 8:30 A.M.–5:00 P.M.)

ADK is a nonprofit, tax-exempt organization. Membership fees are tax deductible, as allowed by law. Please allow 6-8 weeks for receipt of first issue of *Adirondac*.

CDH

ADK Publications

FOREST PRESERVE SERIES

1 Adirondack Mountain Club High Peaks Trails
2 Adirondack Mountain Club Eastern Trails
3 Adirondack Mountain Club Central Trails
4 Adirondack Mountain Club Western Trails
5 Adirondack Mountain Club Northville–Placid Trail
6 Adirondack Mountain Club Catskill Trails

OTHER TITLES

Adirondack Alpine Summits: An Ecological Field Guide
Adirondack Birding: 60 Great Places to Find Birds
Adirondack Canoe Waters: North Flow
Adirondack Mountain Club Canoe and Kayak Guide: East-Central New York State
Adirondack Mountain Club Canoe Guide to Western & Central New York State
Adirondack Paddling: 60 Great Flatwater Adventures
An Adirondack Sampler I: Day Hikes for All Seasons
Catskill Day Hikes for All Seasons
Forests and Trees of the Adirondack High Peaks Region
Kids on the Trail! Hiking with Children in the Adirondacks
No Place I'd Rather Be: Wit and Wisdom from Adirondack Lean-to Journals
Ski and Snowshoe Trails in the Adirondacks
The Adirondack Reader
The Catskill 67: A Hiker's Guide to the Catskill 100 Highest Peaks under 3500'
Views from on High: Fire Tower Trails in the Adirondacks and Catskills
Winterwise: A Backpacker's Guide

MAPS

Trails of the Adirondack High Peaks Region
Northville-Placid Trail
Trails Illustrated Map 742: Lake Placid/High Peaks
Trails Illustrated Map 743: Lake George/Great Sacandaga
Trails Illustrated Map 744: Northville/Raquette Lake
Trails Illustrated Map 745: Old Forge/Oswegatchie
Trails Illustrated Map 746: Saranac/Paul Smiths
Trails Illustrated Map 755: Catskill Park

ADIRONDACK MOUNTAIN CLUB CALENDAR
price list available upon request

The Adirondack Mountain Club, Inc.
Orders only: 800-395-8080 (Mon.–Sat., 8:30–5:00)
www.adk.org

Index

Locations are listed by proper name with *Lake* or *Mount* following.

Acra Point and Burnt Knob, 55–56
    map, 51
Adirondack Mountains, contrasted to
    Catskills, 28
Alder Lake, 139, 142
    map, 116
animals, wild, 22–23
arboretum, 32
archery season, 22
Artists Rock, 36–37
Ashokan High Point, 129, 131
    map, 130
Ashokan Reservoir, 101
    map, 102
autumn, 26. *See also* hunting season

Badman Cave, 41
Balsam Lake Mountain Loop, 140–141
    map, 138
Balsam Mountain Loop, 109, 111
    map, 110
Batavia Kill Day-Use Area, 49
Beach, Charles, 43, 45
Bearpen Mountain, 158, 160
    map, 159
bears
    dangers of, 22
    food and, 22, 25–26
    hunting season for, 22
Beaverkill Covered Bridge, 139
Beaverkill Public Campground, 139
Beaverkill Trout Hatchery, 139
Becker Hollow, 73
    map, 70
Belleayre Beach, 103
Belleayre Mountain, 103, 104, 106
    map, 105
berries, 26
Biscuit Brook Bushwhack, 131, 133
    map, 132
black bears, *see* bears
Black Dome Mountain, 49–50
    map, 51
blackflies, 25
Blackhead Mountain Loop, 52–53
    map, 51

Blackhead Range and Northern
Escarpment, 49
    Acra Point and Burnt Knob, 51,
        55–56
    Black Dome Mountain, 49–51
    Blackhead Mt. Loop, 51, 52–53
    Camels Hump, 51, 53–54
    Dutcher Notch from Colgate Lake,
        60, 61–62
    Stoppel Point, 59–61
    Windham High Peak, 56–59

blue line, 14, 29
bluestone, 28, 100
body temperature, safety and, 17–18
body waste, 21
boots, 19, 27
Boulder Rock and Split Rock Loop,
    34–36
    map, 30
Brinks, Jacob, 85
Burnt Knob, 55–56
    map, 51
Burroughs, John, 119–120, 157
    memorial field, 157
    memorial plaque, 108, 121
    quotes, 31, 49, 63, 85, 103, 119,
        139, 157

Cables Lake, *see* Trout Pond
Camels Hump, 53–54
    map, 51
campgrounds
    in East Catskills, 85
    in Northeast Catskills, 31, 37
    in South Catskills, 120
    in Southwest Catskills, 139
carry it in, carry it out policy, 23
Cathedral Glen Loop, 106–107
    map, 105
Catskill Fly Fishing Center and
    Museum, 140
Catskill Center for Conservation and
    Development, 103
Catskill Mt. House, 31, 34–35, 45, 46

Catskill Mt. House and Lakeside
  Loop, 47–48
  map, 30
Catskill Mt. Railroad, 85, 120
Catskill Mts., 28–29
Catskill Park, 29
Catskill State Fish Hatchery, 139
cellular telephones, dangers of
  reliance on, 16

Central Catskills, 103
  Belleayre Mt., 104–106
  Cathedral Glen Loop, 105, 106–107
  Kelly Hollow, 115–117
  Lookouts on Dry Brook Ridge,
    113–115
  Rider Hollow Trail and Balsam Mt.
    Loop, 109–111
  Rochester Hollow, 105, 108
  Seager Trail to Waterfalls, 110–112

children, hiking with, 23–24, 26
clothing
  recommendations, 18–19
  for specific seasons, 25–27
Cole, Thomas, 54
Colgate Lake, 32
  Dutcher Notch from, 60, 61–62
Colonels Chair Trail to Hunter Mt.
  Summit, 71–72
  map, 70
Cornell-Wittenberg-Slide Loop from
  Woodland Valley, 125–126
  map, 118
covered bridges, 139, 140, 148–150
Covered Bridge Trek to Waterfall, 148,
  150
  map, 149
Coykendall Lodge, 142
crampons, 26
Curtis, William, 122
Curtis-Ormsbee Trail, 120–122
  map, 118

Dannys Lookout, 74–75
  map, 70
deer season, 21–22
Delaware and Ulster Rail Ride, 103
Department of Environmental
  Conservation (DEC), emergency
  numbers for, 18

Devils Path Peaks, 63
  Becker Hollow, 70, 73
  Colonels Chair Trail to Hunter Mt.
    Summit, 70–72
  Diamond Notch Falls and
    Diamond Notch, 65, 72–73
  Hunter Mt. Loops from Spruceton
    Valley and from Stony Clove, 67–70
  Indian Head Mt. Loop, 79, 81–83
  Magical Quarry on Sugarloaf,
    77–79
  Orchard Point and Dannys
    Lookout, 70, 74–75
  Sugarloaf Mt. Loop, 75–77, 79
  Twin Mt. from Pecoy Notch and
    Jimmy Dolan Notch, 78–81
  West Kill Mt., 64–66

Devils Tombstone, 63
Diamond Notch Falls and Diamond
  Notch, 72–73
  map, 65
Dry Brook Ridge, lookouts on, 113, 115
  map, 114
Dry Brook Ridge Trail, 141
Dunn, John, 27
Dutcher Notch from Colgate Lake,
  61–62
  map, 60

East Ashokan Lookout, 131
East Catskills, 85
  Ashokan Reservoir, 101–102
  Echo Lake and Overlook Mt. from
    Platte Clove, 84, 93, 94–96
  Huckleberry Point, 84, 87–88
  Kaaterskill High Peak, 84, 86–87
  Mount Tremper from Willow, 96–98
  Onteora Lake, 98–100
  Overlook Mt. from Woodstock,
    91–94
  Poets Ledge and Wildcat Falls,
    89–91

Echo Lake and Overlook Mt. from
  Platte Clove, 94–96
  maps, 84, 93
Elm Ridge Trail, 58–59
emergency telephone numbers, 18
Empire State Railway Museum, 85, 120

equipment
  for feet, 19, 26, 27
  list of recommended, 21
  for specific seasons, 25–27
  whistles, 24
Esopus Creek, tubing on, 85, 120
Evers, Alf, 19
Evers, Christopher, 19

fires, safety and, 21
fire towers
  in Central Catskills, 104, 106
  in East Catskills, 94, 96, 98
  information about renovated, 17
  in Northeast Catskills, 69
  in South Catskills, 133, 135
  in Southwest Catskills, 140–141
first aid, 19, 21
Fish, Pete, 128, 135
fish hatcheries, 139, 142
fly fishing museum, 140
food
  bears and, 22, 25–26
  recommended, 19
footgear, 19, 26–27
Forest Preserve, 14, 29, 63
Frick Pond Loop, 147–148
  map, 146
frostbite, 26–27
Frost Valley YMCA, 120
funicular, 31, 35, 43

gear, see equipment
Giant Ledge, 122–123
  map, 118
Global Positioning System (GPS),
  dangers of reliance on, 16
Great Train Robbery, The (film), 63
Great Wall of Manitou, 28, 29, 31

Harding, George, 45
Harding Road Trail, 44
Harriman Expedition, 119
hatcheries, 139, 142
heat exhaustion, 17–18
heat stroke, 18
High Peaks Interpretive Trail, 106
  map, 105
Huckleberry Point, 87–88
  map, 84

Hudson River Valley Lookout, 33–34
  map, 30
Hunter Lake, 32
Hunter Mt.
  Colonels Chair Trail to, 70–72
  Sky Ride at, 32
Hunter Mt. Loops from Spruceton
  Valley and from Stony Clove, 67–69
  map, 70
Hunter Mt. Ski Museum, 32
hunting season, 21–22
hypothermia, 17, 26

Indian Head Mt. Loop, 81–83
  map, 79
Inspiration Point and Hudson River
  Valley Lookout, 33–34
  map, 30

Jimmy Dolan Notch, 78, 80–81
  map, 79
John Burroughs Memorial Field, 157

Kaaterskill Falls, 46–47
  map, 30
Kaaterskill High Peak, 86–87
  map, 84
Kaaterskill Hotel, 45
Karma Triyana Dharmachaka
  Monastery, 85, 92, 120
Kelly Hollow, 115, 117
  map, 116
Kenneth L. Wilson Campground, 85,
  120

Lakeside Loop, 47–48
  map, 30
Layman, Frank, 33
Leave No Trace program, 20
litter, 20, 23
Little Pine Orchard Picnic Area, 42–43
  map, 40
Little Pond Public Campground, 139
Little Pond to Touchmenot Mt. View,
  143, 145
  map, 144
Livingston Manor Covered Bridge
  Park, 140
Long Pond–Beaver Kill Ridge Trail, 147
Lookouts on Dry Brook Ridge, 113, 115
  map, 114

Lyme disease, 23

Magical Quarry on Sugarloaf, 77–78
  map, 79
maps, legend for, 15–16
Marys Glen Trail, 39, 41
Mary Smith Hill, 151, 153–154
  map, 152
Mill Brook Bridge Trail, 141
Mine Hollow Trail, 111
monastery, 85, 92, 120
Mongaup-Hardenburgh Trail, 145–147
Mongaup Pond and Mt., 145, 147
  map, 146
Mongaup Pond Public Campground, 139
mosquitoes, 25
Mt. House Road, 42
Mountaintop Arboretum, 32
Mud Pond, 154, 156
  map, 155
museums
  Catskill Fly Fishing Center and
    Museum, 140
  Empire State Railway Museum, 85, 120
  Hunter Mt. Ski Museum, 32
  Roscoe O. and W. Railway
    Museum, 140
  Woodstock Historical Society
    Museum, 85, 120
  Zadock Pratt Museum, 158
music festival, 103

narrow-gauge railroad, 31, 42, 63, 68
Newmans Ledge, 36–38
  map, 40
Northeast Catskills, see Blackhead
  Range and Northern Escarpment;
  Devil's Path Peaks; North-South
  Lake and Palenville Area
Northern Escarpment, see Blackhead
  Range and Northern Escarpment
North Point Loop, 38–39, 41
  map, 40
North-South Lake and Palenville
  Area, 31–32
  Boulder Rock and Split Rock Loop,
    30, 34–36
  Catskill Mt. House and Lakeside
    Loop, 30, 47–48

Inspiration Point and Hudson
  River Valley Lookout, 30, 33–34
Kaaterskill Falls, 30, 46–47
North Point Loop, 38–41
Palenville Overlook from Palenville
  and from South Lake, 30, 43–46
Sleepy Hollow Trail to Little Pine
  Orchard Picnic Area, 40, 42–43
Sunset Rock and Newmans Ledge,
  36–38, 40

North-South Lake campground, 32,
  35, 37, 39, 48

Northwest Catskills, 157–158
  Bearpen Mt., 158–160
  Pratt Rock Park, 159–161

Notch Lake, 32

Onteora Lake, 98, 100
  map, 99
Orchard Point and Dannys Lookout,
  74–75
  map, 70
Ormsbee, Allen, 122
Ormsbee-Curtis Trail, 120–122
  map, 118
Overlook Lodge
  High Peaks Interpretive Trail from,
    105, 106
  Peekamoose Trail to, 126–128
Overlook Mt. and Echo Lake from
  Platte Clove, 94–96
  maps, 84, 93
Overlook Mt. from Woodstock,
  91–92, 94
  map, 93
Overlook Mt. House, 92

Palenville Area, see North-South Lake
  and Palenville Area
Palenville Overlook from Palenville
  and from South Lake, 43–46
  map, 30
Pauls Lookout, 122
Peekamoose Trail to Overlook Ledge,
  126, 128
  map, 127
Pine Hill Day-Use Area, 103

Platte Clove, Echo Lake and Overlook
    Mt. from, 94–96
    maps, 84, 93
Poets Ledge and Wildcat Falls, 89, 91
    map, 90
porcupines, 22
Pratt, Zadock, 160–161
Pratt Rock Park, 160–161
    map, 159
private land, respecting, 14

quarries, 77–78, 95–96

rabies, 23
race, at Acra Point, 55
railroads
    Catskill Mt. Railroad, 85, 120
    Delaware and Ulster Rail Ride, 103
    Empire State Railway Museum, 85,
        120
    old narrow-gauge, 31, 42, 63, 68
    Roscoe O. and W. Railway
        Museum, 140
Reconnoiter Rock, 128
Red Falls, 158
Red Hill, 133, 135
    map, 134
Red Hill Fire Tower Committee, 135
Rider Hollow Trail and Balsam Mt.
    Loop, 109, 111
    map, 110
Rip Van Winkle, Lake, 32
Rip Van Winkle House, 42
Rochester Hollow, 108
    map, 105
Roscoe O. and W. Railway Museum,
    140

safety issues
    body temperature, 14, 17
    children and, 24
    equipment, 21
    fires, 21
    first aid, 19, 21
    hiking out, 17–18
    Lyme disease, 23
    physical conditioning, 18
    rabies, 23
    in specific seasons, 25–27
    wildlife, 22–23

Seager Trail to Waterfalls, 111–112
    map, 110
seasons, 25–27
sedimentary rock, 28, 100
Shermans Lookout, 82
Shorey, A.T., 31
ski lift, see Sky Rides
ski museum, 32
Sky Rides
    Belleayre Mt., 103
    Hunter Mt., 32, 71
Sleepy Hollow–Harding Road Loop, 45
Sleepy Hollow Trail to Little Pine
    Orchard Picnic Area, 42–43
    map, 40
Slide Mt., 118–122, 125–126
Slide Mt. Loop via Curtis-Ormsbee
    Trail, 120–122
    map, 118
Slide-Wittenberg-Cornell Loop from
    Woodland Valley, 125–126
    map, 118
snakes, 22–23
snowshoes, 26
snowmobile trail, 147
socks, 19, 27

South Catskills, 119–120
    Ashokan High Point, 129–131
    Biscuit Brook Bushwhack, 131–133
    Giant Ledge, 118, 122–123
    Peekamoose Trail to Overlook
        Ledge, 126–128
    Red Hill, 133–135
    Slide Mt. Loop via Curtis-Ormsbee
        Trail, 118, 120–122
    Vernooy Kill Falls, 135–137
    Wittenberg-Cornell-Slide Loop
        from Woodland Valley, 118,
        125–126
    Wittenberg Mt., 118, 123–124

South Lake, Palenville Overlook from,
    45–46
    map, 30

Southwest Catskills, 139–140
    Alder Lake, 142
    Balsam Lake Mt. Loop, 138, 140–141
    Covered Bridge Trek to Waterfall,
        148–150

Frick Pond Loop, 146–148
Little Pond to Touchmenot Mt.
   View, 143–145
Mary Smith Hill, 151–154
Mongaup Pond and Mt., 145–147
Split Rock Lookout, 150–152
Trout Pond and Mud Pond, 154–156

Split Rock Lookout, 150–151
   map, 152
Split Rock Loop, 34–36
   map, 30
spring, 25
Spruceton Valley, Hunter Mt. Loop
   from, 67–69
   map, 70
stagecoaches, 31, 42
Stony Clove, Hunter Mt. Loop from,
   67–69
   map, 70
Stoppel Point, 59, 61
   map, 60
Sugarloaf Mt. Loop, 75–77
   map, 79
summer, 25–26
Sunset Lodge, 106
Sunset Rock and Newmans Ledge,
   36–38
   map, 40

tannin, 28
telephones
   danger of reliance on cellular, 16
   emergency numbers, 18
Thomas Cole Mt., 52, 53, 54
ticks, 23
Touchmenot Mt. View, 143, 145
   map, 144
trail markers, 16–17
Tremper (Mount) from Willow, 96, 98
   map, 97
Trout Pond and Mud Pond, 154, 156
   map, 155
tubing, on Esopus Creek, 85, 120
Twin Mt. from Pecoy Notch and
   Jimmy Dolan Notch, 78, 80–81
   map, 79

Vernooy Kill Falls, 135–136
   map, 137

walking out, 14, 17–18
water, 19
waterfalls
   Buttermilk Falls, 128
   Covered Bridge Trek to, 148–150
   at Diamond Notch, 64, 68, 72
   Kaaterskill Falls, 46–47
   at Kelly Hollow, 117
   at Plattekill Creek, 95
   Red Falls, 158
   Seager Trail to, 112
   Vernooy Kill Falls, 135–136
   Wildcat Falls, 91
weather
   safety issues, 17
   in specific seasons, 25–27
West Kill Mt., 64, 66
   map, 65
whistle, carrying, 24
wildlife, 22–23
Windham High Peak, 56–59
   loop option, 56
   map, 57
winter, 26–27
Winterwise: A Backpacker's Guide
   (Dunn), 27
Wittenberg-Cornell-Slide Loop from
   Woodland Valley, 125–126
   map, 118
Wittenberg Mt., 123–124
   map, 118
Woodchuck Lodge, 157–158
Woodstock Historical Society
   Museum, 85, 120

YMCA, in Frost Valley, 120

Zadock Pratt Museum, 158